JANE TIERNEY

TŌBŌ

One woman's escape

Futura

For Barney with love
malgré tout

A Futura Book

Copyright © 1985 by Jane Tierney

First published in Great Britain in 1985
Judy Piatkus (Publishers) Ltd, London

This edition published in 1986
by Futura Publications, a Division of
Macdonald & Co (Publishers) Ltd
London & Sydney

ISBN 0 7088 3046 3

Printed and bound in Great Britain by
Collins, Glasgow

Futura Publications
A Division of
Macdonald & Co (Publishers) Ltd
Greater London House
Hampstead Road
London NW1 7QX

A BPCC plc Company

Jane Tierney was born in Staffordshire, the younger sister of two brothers. She endured what she describes as a very tough upbringing in her male dominated family and is convinced that this gave her the tough constitution which in later life helped her to survive exceptional traumas and extreme circumstances.

She was educated first of all at Wycombe Abbey and later, from the age of 14, in Paris. She is fluent in French and has also lived in many other parts of the world including the Middle East, Persia and America.

Jane Tierney is an experienced and highly qualified pilot with 1700 hours recorded flying time. Her passionate hobby has been the writing of a fully comprehensive history of scents and perfume, a work to which she has long been devoted.

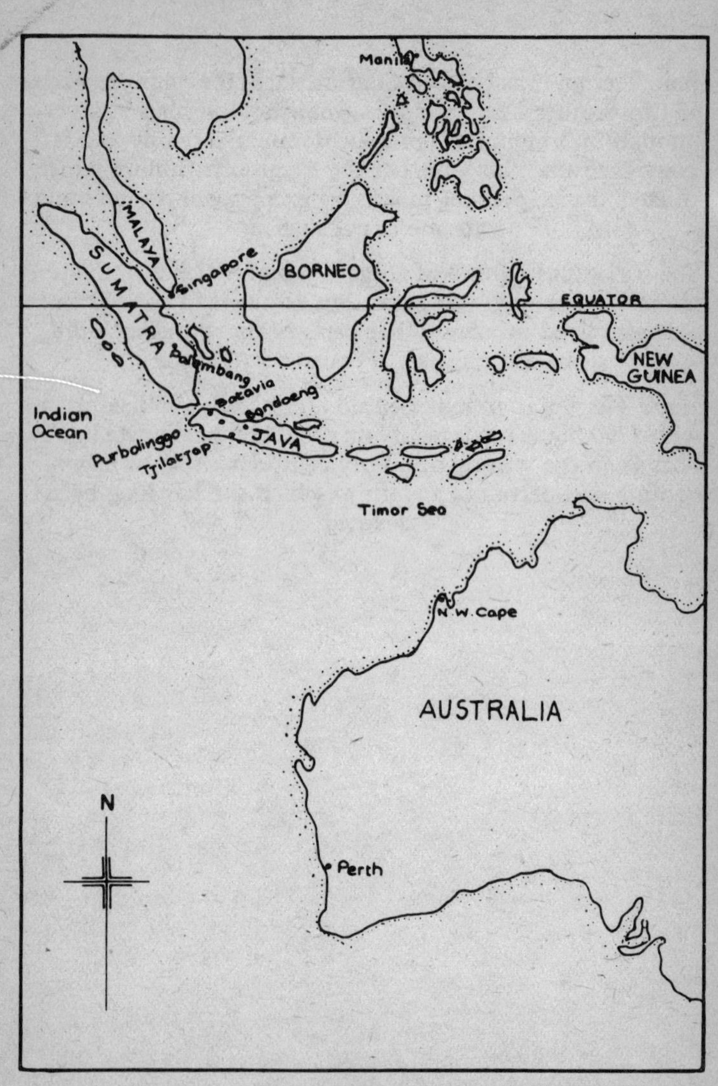

Manila
MALAYA
SUMATRA
Singapore
BORNEO
EQUATOR
NEW GUINEA
Palembang
Batavia
Bandoeng
Indian Ocean
Purbolinggo
Tjilatjap
JAVA
Timor Sea
N.W. Cape
AUSTRALIA
N
Perth

ONE

Where to begin? What to put? It all began, I suppose, the first time I saw Morgan.

It was evening early in 1939 in the Flying Club at Shoreham-by-Sea. The Club was the 'in' place that winter, along that part of the south coast. We were all very much aware that war with Germany was imminent. Everybody was on their toes. A lot of people were already rearranging their lives. A time of hardship was inevitably coming and had to be dealt with.

Morgan was holding forth to a group near the bar, a ruggedly good-looking, blue-eyed man in one of those expensive brightly patterned Fair Isle jerseys that make any man look attractive.

But he was different. One of the first things I noticed was the odd way he had of holding his cigarette and of throwing away a match. He held the stick between thumb and long middle finger and flicked it like an arrow straight into an ashtray yards away. I tried it myself when I got home and almost set fire to the cat.

The next morning, he was there again, in Air Force uniform and in the evening in drab grey. Old trousers, sweater, shirt, everything iron grey. Only someone really full of himself would wear such a boring colour and get away with it, I thought.

This time I was nearer and listened unashamedly to his voice. He was telling a far-fetched story in an Irish accent about some boxers in a pub, but I didn't understand the punch line.

A plump girl with hair like a pile of sausages asked him what he did.

'Intrepid aviator, of course,' he replied, looking down her cleavage. Anyone else saying a thing like that would sound a right idiot, but not him, I thought. He would never look a fool, whatever he did. I made an ass of myself every time I opened my mouth, but he had it all worked out. I listened some more. He certainly knew what to say, but mostly it was a question of knowing what not to say. I had heard there were people like that.

One of the instructors told a very short, very dirty and unfunny story, and the girl shrieked. The man in grey said nothing but conveyed by the expression in his hooded eyes, the patient half-smile about the mouth, that he felt only contempt but was too well-bred to put it into words.

Then, he looked directly across at me.

Our involvement was immediate and intense. From the moment my eyes met his searching blue ones, I was in love.

Gauche, self-conscious, tongue-tied, suddenly to the exclusion of all else, I wanted to please him.

In a wild effort to be intriguing I began talking in an affected French accent, like the new lead last week at the Rep.

'You want to be careful – it might stick, see!' he whispered for my ears only, in a Welsh sing-song. 'From the Black Country you come – isn't it?' he persisted.

I should have been furious but I wasn't. I just agreed that he was right and knocked my cup of coffee straight into my lap.

Everybody laughed but Morgan. He mopped me up and got me a fresh cup. Then he came and sat next to me and asked me about my flying course. I told him that I wasn't very good and about dropping the Tiger Moth from about six feet a few days before. He said that that was pretty traditional and not to be bothered about and that what I needed was a bit of help and a lot of looking after.

He drove me home, or at least to my aunt's house where I was staying while I was on the course. Going through the villages some houses were already completely blacked out, others had chinks of light where the black-out curtains were inadequate, some were in the process of being installed. There was a great air of tension. Before he dropped me in my aunt's garage yard, he held me very close and said, 'You are rare and beautiful and I want you.'

Five days and four sleepless nights later, he asked me to marry him. I said yes. He was always right about everything and unfailingly right about me. Everything that had gone before was of no importance. When I met him, my life began. He made it plain that he really needed me.

My family home was at Tettenhall in Staffordshire near the Shropshire border. I was brought up rather strictly with two brothers six and eight years older than me. I was a very naughty child, a rebel, constantly being scolded and punished by my mother who liked the boys better than me. I was my father's favourite. When I reached about eighteen my mother was jealous of his pride in me.

The first thing I remember being whipped for, was for eating the chickens' food. Bran and potato peelings. I liked it so much more than porridge or semolina pudding.

Sent away to boarding school at twelve, I was wretched and suffered unutterable longings for the holidays and to be with the boys again. Although so much younger I persisted in tagging along everywhere with them and I believe this tough rugged training toughened me up for physical hardships later in life.

In the long summer holidays we used to get up at about five o'clock in the mornings and climb through my bedroom window, slithering down the roof of the woodshed to the ground.

We raided neighbours' strawberry beds, apple orchards and let rabbits out of their hutches. We drummed up gang warfare sorties, sometimes as pirates, sometimes as secret servicemen.

A few miles across the fields behind our house was an old manor house in ruins called Dunstall Hall. It had a moat.

My brothers could jump this at its narrowest part and I always had a go but never made it. I fell in backwards every time and always arrived home soaking wet. Some of our more daring escapades bordered on delinquency.

I learned to skate before I was six and fell through thin ice several times. It was never possible to go home and have a hot bath because our old-fashioned plumbing was always frozen solid in skating weather.

My front teeth were knocked out by a cricket ball before their natural time and I was shot through the left cheek by a sago ball fired from an air-gun wielded by my elder brother whom I hero-worshipped. It left a nasty beetroot-coloured blemish which I tried to cover for years after I grew up, until I met a clever Frenchwoman who taught me to darken and emphasise the mark, turning it into a beauty spot.

My elder brother was a marvellous character – my guide and mentor. It was he who explained to me the facts of life, very clearly and beautifully; and when I started my periods and thought myself stricken with a fatal disease, he calmed me gently, telling me that I had become a woman and should be proud.

When he was twenty-one and in his second year at Oxford he took me for a walking-tour in the Cotswolds. He gave me the right books to read, grew angry if he caught me reading trash, and read poetry to me in the evenings. He was a brilliant scholar and later, at the early age of thirty-five became Headmaster of Harrow. Sadly, he died of cancer ten years later.

I had grown up feeling a deprived abnormal child because, although my brothers suffered all the usual childish diseases, I never caught anything and was boarded out with a horrid woman in the village called Mrs Carrington. She looked evil with her dyed very black hair, and eyes too close together. She always wore tight corsets and black cotton dresses – all ribs and cloth like an umbrella.

Once, I locked her in the cellar but let her out after a while because I began feeling sorry for the mice. No tea or supper for me that day.

I used to jump out of bed early every morning of my banishment to examine my face for spots but there never were any. Nor were there any get-well cards and presents like the boys had. It simply wasn't fair.

Quite early on I acquired the reputation of being a 'bolter'. I ran away from school but was taken straight back the next day. I ran away from Mrs Carrington's and lived in the chicken shed for two days. I always left dull girls' parties and went to the tram depot to watch the trams turn around.

When I was fourteen, my mother decided to send me to school in Paris. I was entered in a *cours* near the Parc Monceau and lived with family friends of my mother's on the Boulevard Courcelles.

I enjoyed my time in France and at the end of my last term got myself an interview with Maggy Rouff, a famous couturier of the time. The Grande Dame warned me I would be picking up pins and making coffee during the first year and then I might move to the *toiles* (patterns) room. I didn't care. I intended to become a great dressmaker and designer.

My family, however, thought otherwise and my father, usually so indulgent and understanding, came and dragged me home within days.

Again, I ran away. This time in answer to a job for someone to teach French at a co-educational school. It turned out to be the first Bertrand Russell school at Beacon Hill on the South Downs.

It was the oddest place. The children were in no way disciplined and wore common clothing – that is they helped themselves to whatever they fancied from a huge clothes closet.

I soon found that I not only had to teach French – if anyone turned up to listen – but had to do a lot of menial tasks. This included catching the unbroken ponies – most of them wild from Exmoor – for the spoiled little brats to ride, and breaking ice for the ponies to drink on winter mornings. I stayed there a year.

It was one day while lying in the coarse grass of Chanctonbury Ring looking up at the sky I first noticed a small aircraft. All that perfect unblemished blue sky and one small speck free to go wherever it wished.

Maybe all too soon the skies would be full of aircraft. I felt I would like to be part of it. At least I could learn to work in an aircraft factory or join the WAAF.

Suddenly I was lifted from black despair into freedom. Just

by looking into the sky I felt I must be in it. Touch it I don't care, I thought, I'm happy. I am going to learn to fly.

I had saved almost all my pay from the teaching job and wrote to my father appealing for a loan. It was unfortunately at a time when his wrought-iron business was not going too well, but he said he would think about it.

As soon as I got home, I went to work on him. Fondly appealing, even offering to go with him to some boring local art exhibition of wishy-washy works done by local ladies, I could see he was going to help me. So, the next afternoon, I put on his favourite white dress and tied back my hair with a ribbon to match my eyes. He told me he was proud of me. I even peered at the exhibits and smarmed some of the old dears.

As we were leaving, I said, 'Don't you think it would be nice to take some flowers home for Mother?' He agreed and from a near-by florist he bought a huge posy, big as a cauliflower, of Parma violets (whatever happened to Parma violets?).

When he handed them to her, she took the neat bouquet and bashed it against the edge of the dining-room table. Pale lilac-coloured heads flew in all directions and the bruised bundle of stalks fell to the carpet. I began feverishly picking up the poor severed heads but my father said, 'Leave them, go up to your room, your mother and I want to talk.'

Sometime later, he came up to see me and said I must not be upset by the scene I had witnessed downstairs. 'No marriage – indeed life itself – is ever plain sailing, you know. When you are older you will understand. Now, what's all this about learning to fly?'

I explained that I felt I had found my true vocation at last and was determined to follow it. There was a reasonable course offered at Shoreham-by-Sea.

He smiled and said, 'Well, perhaps you could stay with Great-Aunt Edith who lives at Steyning. She's very well-off but must be lonely. I'll give her a ring and sound her out. You'll have to behave yourself, you know. No staying out till all hours –

meanwhile, this is for you, it's about all I can manage at the moment.'

He handed me a thick bundle of crisp, white five-pound notes. I counted them. Two hundred pounds. I flung my arms round his neck and clung to him. 'You are the best father a girl could have,' I said and tears streamed down my face.

'Well, take care and God bless,' he said giving me his handkerchief. 'Better go down and give your mother a hand with supper. Be nice to her,' he added.

Great-Aunt Edith was somewhat guarded in her letter to me in response to my father's call. 'I lead a quiet life and go to bed early. I shall expect you to do the same, within reason, if you are to stay in my house,' she wrote.

My father drove me down to Sussex a few days later. Aunt Edith patted my cheek and said, 'So, our naughty little hooligan has grown into quite a pretty girl. A little more grooming and we might have a beauty in the family yet!'

On 11 October 1938, I climbed into a Tiger Moth for my first lesson. Each lesson lasted half an hour. The first two went without hitch and I was congratulated, then I hit a bad patch and made several terrible landings. I recovered my skills and after nine and a half hours was told I was ready to go solo.

On hearing these words, an excitement that began at the base of my spine and caused flutterings around the ribs rendered me incapable of speech.

I taxied my little biplane across to the start of the rough grass take-off. Taking a long deep breath, all nerves left me. Up there, perched on the edge of a late summer cloud, I looked down over a smooth lettuce-green countryside and felt a supreme triumph and a great peace. Circling the airfield twice, keeping well above Lancing School Chapel spire at 325 feet as instructed, I had to admit that if I never became a great aviator, just being able to be alone in that limitless cool sky would do till something better came along.

A perfect landing, then being surrounded by congratulating instructors was wonderful, but above and beyond all this I had an overwhelming feeling that something lovely was about to happen.

Back in the office I was enrolled at once as a member of the Civil Air Guard to be trained for Air Transport Command. My instructor explained that young weekend fliers and all available amateurs were to be trained specially to enable them to ferry aircraft from factory to airfields around the country. There was a great deal of talent available. I was of course a complete novice, but with enough effort in the space of weeks could become eligible for entry to ATA.

I went back to my aunt's house in seventh heaven. Even my old aunt was interested and enthusiastic over my ambition, and was now prepared to lend me her car unstintingly to go back and forth to Shoreham.

We were married very quietly in a squat small church at Fairford. Morgan had gone back to his bomber-squadron station in Wiltshire, and we had a two-day honeymoon at an hotel in Swindon.

We stayed in bed all day and had our meals sent up and only went out once to feed the ducks with bits of smoked salmon and marzipan off the rather nasty cake Morgan had insisted on buying so that I shouldn't miss out on anything.

It was wonderful. He was so strong and good-looking. He made me feel precious, special and important. I was incandescent, besotted by love and felt like Princess Marina, Lana Turner and Irma La Douce all rolled into one. I used to run my fingers over his forehead, his eyebrows, his lips. There were still so many things I had never dared to say to him yet. Perhaps I never could. His beauty and familiarity made me weak.

I had asked for a week's special leave but I need not have bothered because the weather turned very nasty and all Club flying was cancelled for about ten days.

We left the hotel and went to share a service quarter with a very alcoholic flight-lieutenant and his wife at the Base. Then came the blow. Morgan was posted with his squadron to the Far East.

I knew instantly that somehow I had to follow him. But how?

How could I get out of the Service? Resign for health reasons? Impossible. I was as tough and healthy as a mountain goat. No doctor could find anything wrong with me.

Crash a plane? Probably kill myself? Daft. Land down-wind as if by mistake? Be reprimanded, possibly dismissed. Possible but unlikely. Not conclusive enough.

I had to do something really heinous. I would bounce a landing, deliberately damage the aircraft. Then resign.

So, one cold morning in December flying an Avro-Cadet from airfield to workshops, making a regulation approach landing, I kept the nose much too high and cut the throttle. We must have dropped ten feet. It felt as if the whole machine had fallen to pieces.

In actual fact although we had slewed round and one wing was completely smashed, the fuselage damage was minimal. About two thousand pounds worth, I reckoned. Refusing to talk to anyone, I went into the control tower and wrote my resignation. I wondered if they would make me pay for the damage. If they did – even if it meant robbing a bank – the way I felt about Morgan, I would do it.

I went back to my family and set about finding a job which might enable me to join him. I was incredibly lucky. My resignation was accepted and that same day a chance meeting with a rather snobby friend of my mother's led me to her son-in-law who worked in the French Embassy.

He was looking for someone married to a member of the Armed Forces (for security reasons) who could read and write fluent French, for a job in Postal Censorship in Singapore. I was, as Morgan often described me to our friends, a bi-lingual illiterate (I couldn't read or write in two languages).

The interview was easy. I was given a bit of a *Times* leader to translate. It was a very high-flown piece about world protein supplies and full of words which I didn't know the meaning of in English. I just wrote what I thought the chap was trying to say into colloquial French and to my amazement my interviewer said '*Excellent*' and started explaining about visas and inoculations. He didn't even really read my translation and all the time kept looking at my legs.

TWO

In March 1940 I went out to Singapore, crossing the unoccupied part of France to catch a P&O boat from Marseilles.

The trip was very slow and I passed the time mugging up some Malay from an ancient phrase book which gave useful sentences such as 'Have the elephants arrived yet?' and 'Can you build me a boat in three days?'

Reading the incredibly lavish menus presented before each meal also took up quite a lot of time. About seven alternatives for each of five courses took a great deal of planning and careful consideration.

There was a young bank clerk from Cardiff on board. He had hair like patent leather and an ingratiating manner, but I started being nicer to him when he told me he knew Morgan.

I had only known him myself for about six weeks. Morgan had told me so little about himself, I was avid for information. The bank clerk told me Morgan was a celebrity. Did I not know that he had played rugby for Wales twice in '37? He was also a heavyweight boxer. He had been educated at Penarth Grammar School and intended on leaving to become a PT instructor but he was so involved with rugby and boxing these sports filled his time until he was accepted into the RAF. Within his first year he became Heavyweight Boxing Champion. He was a celebrity in Cardiff, all right!

A Rugby International and he had never even mentioned it! I felt fit to burst with pride and continued to ply the young man with questions. It seemed Morgan had had to give up boxing when his hands began to show signs of damage. Of course his flying was more important.

I was avid for more and more news of him and asked about his family. Morgan's father, a rather quiet man the young man said, was forester on the Earl of Plymouth's estate at St Fagan's, a small village outside Cardiff. His mother had kept all his rugby caps and shirts and several Victor Ludorum medals won while at school. I sat and glowed with pride.

On the ship were two other young Air Force wives married to men in Morgan's squadron. They looked very smart and sophisticated and made me feel 'country-cousinish'. Their clothes were trendy, even flashy, I thought secretly, and the way they carried on with any men around would have been described by my mother as 'fast'.

I spoke to them a few times. Irene was Canadian with dark curly hair and laughing eyes, and Natalie was tall and slim with ginger hair and hazel eyes. Her features were sharp and when someone told me later that at school she had been nick-named 'Foxy', I was not surprised.

Irene was going to work as a cipher clerk and Natalia had fixed a job to do the social page on a Singapore newspaper. Irene was married to Ross Edwards, a stocky Canadian, and Natalie to Joe Fagan, a tall lanky Irishman with an irrepressible sense of humour.

Both women were wearing 'Wings' brooches – the diamanté kind – too big with brightly coloured bits in the middle. I fingered my own small plain solid gold pin – a parting gift from my brother – and felt constantly grateful for his good taste.

One evening on the ship all three of us were invited to the first-class bar to drink with some men the girls were friendly with. We were given 'Side-Car' cocktails to drink. I didn't care for the taste and after only one, felt quite light-headed and asked for Perrier water. Natalie said I should grow up a bit and have some fun.

Shortly after that remark I retreated to my cabin. I had to share this with a mother and daughter going out to Alexandria where the girl was to meet and marry her fiancé, an army subaltern. The girl was very demure and looked like a Dante Gabriel Rossetti painting with her cloud of dark hair and heart-shaped face. She wore Liberty-print cotton dresses and white lisle stockings.

The mother was even stricter than my own. She dressed and undressed kneeling uncomfortably on her bunk with the curtains drawn closed. After Alexandria I had the cabin blissfully to myself.

There were dances under the starlight, and fierce flirtations flourished on the boat deck. I was contented to lie in my stuffy cabin and think of Morgan.

The ship put into Bombay briefly and we stopped over ashore two nights in Colombo, Ceylon. I was given an enormous bedroom in a posh hotel called the Galle Face, and in what I supposed was the bathroom was confronted with a huge vase about five feet tall full of water. Imagining this to be some eastern sort of bath-tub I scrambled into it and had the utmost difficulty in getting out. Only when I had dried myself did I see a small saucepan-shaped ladle which was obviously intended for baling water over oneself from the jar.

Arriving at the docks in Singapore, Morgan – barely recognisable in baggy khaki shorts and shirt – was there to meet me. Our reunion was somewhat clouded by the pushy young bank clerk but Morgan dealt with him cursorily before leading me over to a rather battered old Austin car. I sat in it obediently while Morgan claimed my trunk and cases and then we drove off towards the town.

The first thing that struck me about Singapore was the dazzling brilliance of all the colours. As it rained for about half an hour each day everything was washed and refreshed so that the flowers, trees and grass looked brand new. It took some getting used to the idea of perpetual regrowth. No seasonal changes. The colours people wore were eye-catchingly brilliant too. Everything was spanking clean, immaculate. The white drill of the serving boys' uniforms was so white it looked almost pale blue.

We were to stay the first few nights with Morgan's CO and his wife. She was Australian and as I had never heard an Australian before I thought her Cockney.

Everything was a bit constrained. I could see Morgan was anxious for me to make a good impression, so I spoke little at lunch; but later at dinner I recounted various incidents that had happened on the boat and my story of climbing into the water-jar raised gales of laughter and I could see Morgan was pleased with me.

It was very kind of the CO and his wife to put us up but I couldn't really relax there – even in bed – for Morgan was apt to make me cry out and squeal and I was aware that we were being overheard. I know Morgan felt the same, too, for the day he came back from the base and said we could move into our own place was sheer magic.

A two-roomed ground-floor flat with rickety bamboo furniture and a lumpy bed, but we couldn't wait to tear our clothes off and make love. Afterwards I had cried with gratitude and the sense of luxury that after all this time he could again really be a part of my body. It seemed too much of a miracle and made the physical pleasure, though keen, almost unimportant. I could hold him in my arms and laugh or cry. I was really reunited with him.

We put on some clothes and inspected the rest of the flat. A kitchen had been rigged up on an open balcony. A row of cats sat on the wall. The so-called bathroom was a lofty kiosk with slimy floor sloping to a drain in the middle. The usual gigantic jar of water and small tin saucepan were the sole furnishings.

All sorts of dark worms and other animals climbed out of the grating and up your legs if you didn't hop about. Morgan said I would make a smashing cabaret turn but I didn't think this very funny.

Morgan went off back to the CO's bungalow to collect the rest of our things and while he was away I tidied myself up, put on some make-up, and brushed my hair into a new shape.

As soon as he got back, I saw from the look in his eye I had been wasting my time. 'This is ridiculous,' I said as he tore off my housecoat and pushed me back onto the rumpled bed, but we made love at once and I was violent and feverish as if there might never be another opportunity. Afterwards we baled water over each other in the grisly bathroom and clung to each other in silence for a few minutes listening to the gurgling drain.

The next day when Morgan went to the airfield at Tengah (his Base), I took a taxi and reported to the French Consulate. To my proposed job working at the postal censorship department, was added the new responsibility of representing General de Gaulle's newly formed Free French Forces. My pay sounded astronomical — more than twice Morgan's — and I was to have a car and *syce* (driver).

The Consul himself, who looked and sounded like Charles Boyer, took me down to the vast building on Collyer Quay where I was to work from 7.30 a.m. each morning until 2 p.m.

I was duly introduced to the British Post Master and to a fat elderly Frenchwoman from whom I was to take over.

I was empowered to offload any sacks of mail from ships or aircraft in transit through Singapore in any direction. I could order the search of anyone's personal papers or brief cases, and hold any mail which was of any importance to the Allies.

It all sounded alarmingly high-powered and a bit over my head but I intended to have a damn good shot at it.

During the second week I made two fine scoops, discovering from family mail the exact whereabouts of the Vichy HQ's Fighter Command in France, and the locations of several main ammunition stores. These pieces of information were of course sent immediately to London, and resulted in many successful pin-point bombing raids by the RAF.

During the third week I decided the noise and racket of the big main office was too distracting, and moved myself and my new assistant into a smaller, quiet office at the back of the building. My assistant, an erudite American-educated Chinese, was called Sammy Koh. He was very well read and spoke immaculate French and English.

Morgan was more and more frequently being sent on trips up country so our times together were short and sporadic.

During one of his longer absences, feeling time on my hands, I volunteered to go to the Radio Station and listen in to Vichy broadcasts from Indo-China, précis any propaganda, and pass it on to the Free French.

One day when I had some free time I went house-hunting and found a charming Chinese bungalow on top of a hill off the road to the Causeway. It had an *attap* roof, a verandah all round, was charmingly furnished and complete with servants. It was airy, oriental and delightful. The servants comprised a cook-boy, a gardener, and a maid who had been trained in the Embassy in Saigon. She could look after any woman expertly. She washed and coiffed my hair, massaged aching necks and shoulders, and washed and pressed all clothes with skill and care.

I had dreaded telling Morgan what I had done and went out to meet him at the Base. To my surprise, he fully approved of the house, but was furious when I told him of the radio work. He called me a phony patriot and said I was wasting my time anyway. When asked to qualify this he clammed up and poured me a stiff drink. The subject was closed.

The blissful days in the sweet house on Bukit Timah Hill – where we had some memorable parties – were all too short, however. For reasons he still would not explain, Morgan had to be away on longer and longer reconnaissance flights, and insisted that we should move down into the town to live in a small chalet in the grounds of a big hotel called the Goodwood Park.

When he was home we went out and entertained quite a lot, living on Pink Gin Pahits and Benzedrine tablets and sometimes went several nights without proper sleep.

I wondered frequently how long this pace could be kept up, and how long before the new threat of Japanese aggression subsided. There were vague rumours of a Japanese landing made on the east coast at Mersing.

We were very hard up. As current Air Force jargon had it, we were 'living in sin' with no marriage allowance, as the approved marriage age for officers stood at thirty. Morgan was twenty-three. He was adamant and pig-headed about the money I earned. I ought to have been cleverer, more provident, but I wasn't. I bought a big flashy car – a big white drop-head coupé with real tan leather upholstery – and frittered the rest away.

I had fond secret day-dreams like Billy Liar, of a cottage in Devon with hollyhocks and children in the garden and scones and strawberry jam for tea. We never actually talked about having a child, but all the time I was scared of getting pregnant knowing I would be shipped off home. We used a thick rubber contraceptive. It was like making love in a plastic boiler suit. We called the thing 'Hubert' and it lived in a gingham bag in the fridge. Casual references to it probably gave the impression we were maintaining a '*ménage à trois*'.

A lodger couldn't have been more damaging. For years afterwards I couldn't think of 'Hubert' without a tremor. Once playing a word association game at a party, confronted with the word 'erotic', I said 'ice-box' and was made to pay a forfeit because I couldn't produce a lucid explanation. Even now I feel tarty in a gingham dress.

Life continued under a lowering war-cloud. 1940 dragged on into 1941 in an air of growing tension. I had been out there about ten months. A story had been circulated that the English in Malaya were totally unconscious of the growing peril surrounding them, and that they were carrying on as if nothing was happening, that they were all caught napping. This is simply not true.

Rubber and tin were now booming. There was great business activity all around, giving a heightened atmosphere of prosperity and optimism, but underneath it all was the knowledge of an almost certain approaching disaster.

Everyone simply went on doing his or her job in the belief that rubber and tin were amongst the most urgently needed assets of the war.

Meanwhile, being glum and pessimistic didn't help matters – no point in not going to parties or the Club. In typical stiff-upper-lip fashion, the British in Malaya continued to go their own way, making corny jokes and asking each other in for a drink.

Another story rumoured is that the military High Command

thought the jungle was impenetrable. They knew perfectly well that this was not so. Their main worry was not whether or not you could penetrate the jungle, but the actual truth that the jungle existed. The main issue was to ensure that the Japanese should not make a landing.

Morgan did his best to keep me cheerful. He clowned and made me laugh and played tricks on me.

One day when I was off-duty in my little chalet the telephone rang and a high falsetto drawling voice said 'Mrs Morgan?' 'Yes,' I answered. 'This is the Governor's wife, Lady Shenton Thomas speaking. I wonder if you would care to come up to the *hice* for a game of tennis?'

Morgan, of course. 'Sod off, you silly old sausage!' I yelled. From the other end of the line came a gasp, a sharp intake of breath, and the line went dead.

As soon as Morgan came home I challenged him.

With raised eyebrows he said, 'Not me, love, I've been flying all morning. My God, it really was the old bag herself. You'll just have to write her an apology!' He then collapsed in helpless laughter while I seethed in agitation. I set to work right away and composed several letters before I was finally satisfied with one and went down to post it right away. I never did get a reply or a game of tennis at Government House.

Next day brought great jubilation and excitement. We heard that Churchill was sending out two great warships to save the situation. He must have realised that the great Naval Base fortress had all its massive guns pointing out to sea. Never had it been envisaged by the politicians that the Japs might invade from the north or north-west. All my staff filled the windows at Collyer Quay and watched the two splendid ships sail in.

The *Prince of Wales* and the *Repulse*. I was impressed. '*Wah*,' all the Chinese shouted.

A few days later they were both sunk. Something was going badly wrong. That same black day I went down to the Kalang airport to meet Morgan back in a civilian plane from a 'special and secret mission'. The AOC himself was there greeting a line of Army and Air Force officers. There was no sign of Morgan.

One of the officers with a curly red beard was staring at me very hard. Soon after the brass hats had passed, he put his head on one side and winked. He had a nice face like Christ in an Oberammergau Passion play. He came over and put his arms around me. I was livid. I had been fooled again, but I'd know the smell of him in Hell.

The next morning he was sent with the squadrons to Sumatra, which was one of the islands of the Dutch East Indies. He was to command Palembang near the south-west tip of the island where all the big oil storage tanks were positioned. He had been made an Acting Wing-Commander!

I watched the Blenheim bombers fly off and glowed with pride.

I assumed they were off for a short tour of duty and would be back within a few days. Morgan, of course, never talked about his job and since he refused to take mine seriously, I never talked about mine. Maybe my work was not of outstanding importance in the war effort, but I did nevertheless sift many scoops of vital information all told – in particular, discovering exact locations of Nazi strongholds in occupied France, a great deal of information concerning movements of French naval vessels, and the loyalties or otherwise of those in command during the complex Dakar affair.

On 8 December 1941 I was invited to a party at the Swimming Club. It was a good party. We were all having a final swim in the early hours of the morning when we heard bombers overhead.

There was a wild drumming in the air, growing and growing. 'They are having quite an exercise tonight,' I said but the planes didn't sound like Blenheims.

In a very few minutes, something happened which made it quite clear that this was no exercise: thin streams of tracer shots streaked the black sky overhead and bombs started falling in the direction of the town. We grabbed our clothes and sheltered in a cellar. When the raid was over we drove home in the grey dawn shocked into sober silence. There was a sizeable crater in Beach Road and parts of the buildings in Raffles Square were missing. Over the radio we heard of the terrible attack on Pearl Harbor.

'War!' I said out loud. 'So this is it!'

It somehow seemed incongruous in a place where people wore such silly hats.

Next day a rumour went round that the Japanese were using gas, but the people writhing about and choking in the street were found to be suffering nothing worse than ammonia fumes from a cold storage plant that had been hit.

Occasionally, either Natalie or Irene – the wives from the ship – would come and seek me out, but I always felt we had little in common. I think they had more regard for me when they learned of my high-powered job and saw me in lovely new dresses. They lived such very different lives from mine, it was not surprising we had so little in common. I enjoyed the times when we all went out in a sixsome with Joe and Ross and Morgan, but they also went out on dates with other men when their husbands were away. This was something I simply could not do. I only enjoyed drinking and dancing with Morgan, so there was no point in pretending otherwise. They continued to nag me about being stupid and narrow-minded but this didn't worry me.

Few letters from my family at home got through to me. One in particular, from my father, told me that his foundry had been turned over to the Government and now manufactured shells and bomb cases. My father now designed weapons instead of gates and bridges. My mother, who was an excellent cook, was making supper five nights a week for the Air Raid Precaution squads of the neighbourhood, and everyone was very short of food. My father said it was because the German boats in the Channel were sinking so many of our ships carrying imported food supplies. He himself was in charge of a team of ARP officers, each of whom did several all-night stints each week. My elder brother had been made Headmaster of Bristol Grammar School where they were constantly under attack by incendiary bombs.

I felt sad and worried about them and guilty that we were living on the most luxurious foodstuffs while they were deprived. (We had expected shortages after war with Japan was officially declared, but there were none.) The only cheering item was that my old cat Mrs Tibbs had produced three more kittens and all were spoken for.

The day after receiving my father's letter, Irene turned up, looking far from well with puffy eye-lids. She told me she was pregnant and I congratulated her and said how thrilled Ross must be. She shocked me by blurting out that the baby was not his. I jumped to the conclusion it must be one of the Americans I had seen her about with, but even more confusion followed when she told me the child was Joe's, her friend's husband.

She had spent a week-end with him while Ross was up-country, and Natalie was over in Borneo for her paper. She begged me to help her get an abortion but I begged her to put this idea right out of her head and get her name down for a place on the next evacuee ship. Far the best thing to do would be to go home to her family, and after the baby was born and the war was over, there would be time for reconciliations and explanations all round. To my surprise she hugged me and proceeded to take my advice.

About that time I underwent some odd experiences myself. One afternoon I had been doing an extra stint at the Listening-Post, and with head-phones on I was oblivious to the Alert siren. In broad daylight after leaving the office, I came out of the building to find an uncanny silence and no-one moving. Driving along the coast road I came to a group of *attap*-roofed huts and stalls which had been bombed and looked like a giant game of Spillikins. It was horrible. There was no sign of life.

I didn't know whether to stop or go on and then I saw it. The body of a little girl – like a Chinese doll with silver bracelet round one chubby ankle below miniature pyjama – and no head. The head with its tuft of black hair was yards away and bloody.

An ambulance arrived and some Malay police on motor-bikes. One of them waved me on. During the next weeks, I saw many mutilated bodies and some dead, but it was always the child with the severed head who stopped me sleeping and haunted my dreams.

My neighbour at the hotel, occupying the next chalet, was a nervous girl called Grace Caraway. She was terrified of being left alone at night. I undertook to go and sleep in her husband's bed every Friday night when he was on duty at the Naval Base. The arrangement worked well for several weeks until the night I had to stay extra late at the Radio Station.

Crawling into my bed, exhausted, a flash of uneasiness had me wide awake and, realising it was a Friday, I got to my feet, found the right key, pulled a coat on over my nightgown and hurried out down the path. Without putting on any lights I tip-toed into the Caraways' place and looked in. In a shaft of moonlight I could see fat Gracie lying like a clubbed seal.

Parting the mosquito-netting of the other bed, I crawled in and instantly froze. There was a body there already. Arms reached out like tentacles and I shrivelled away to do some calculations. It wasn't Friday. It was Thursday. Jack was home.

I backed out of the bungalow on all fours and got away without waking either of them. I couldn't wait to tell Morgan – but I never did. The right moment never came.

Jack was killed a few days later and Gracie was evacuated. I heard later that she married a Jehovah's Witness, and he certainly wouldn't have thought it funny.

Large-scale evacuation of Service wives and families was now going on. I wasn't particularly worried. Morgan would be back soon. Whenever I was off duty I waited at the chalet or in the hotel near the telephone in case there was a message from him. He filled every waking thought.

I had kept all the letters he had ever written to me, and during those days I used to get them out and read them over and over. After a while I knew from the colour of the envelope, the pictures on the stamps, which contained the phrases I loved best.

'There is so much in this love of ours. One day we will begin to live and life will be very beautiful – very tranquil.'

'Blessed darling – you say, would I come to you if you were another man's wife. Oh darling! I would do anything – you know that. I couldn't live without you, so I would kidnap you and we would collect the insurance on your husband's policy.'

'I shall never get over being away from you now. Every morning when I wake and you are not there, I think of the long hard meaningless day in front of me – I close my eyes and know the shape of you – I can feel the softness of your hair – the touch of you – the smell of your skin. I open my eyes and the emptiness is unbearable.'

'After the war I shall become a churchwarden and settle down with you and pinch the bottoms of young women in the front pew and you will poke me with your umbrella and hold hands on the other side with a very handsome young man. I shall pretend I don't mind and kill him while you are fumbling for your collection – '

'I shall have a little sing now because there might be a letter from you tomorrow.'

Like all Welshmen, Morgan loved to sing. He described his voice as a good pub tenor. It was very powerful. Sometimes to please me he would imitate Richard Tauber and sing through his nose with a German intonation until I fell about with laughing.

He was a born showman, a sort of one-man theatre. Irrelevant absurd remarks in his rich Welsh accent would break the composure of the starchiest people: '*Duw mun*! – Bronwen's pregnant again, then!' or 'No, I tell a lie, it was the day we had fish!'

He was big and incredibly strong with a real superman's physique, massive shoulders, a narrow waist and the legs of a long-distance runner. When they played silly games in the Mess on guest nights, it always used to be one squadron versus Morgan's squadron – but *without* Morgan, for he could pick a man up easily by the seat of his pants with one hand and lift him off the floor.

He was generous, hearty, uninhibited, tough and sentimental.

He never cavilled over petty things, gave people the benefit of the doubt, and drank a lot of beer. Once when we were first married he gave his last fiver away to an airman who had missed his last train, so that he could get a taxi back to camp and avoid possible court-martial.

One day, he led me into an insurance broker's office and solemnly tried to insure my legs. Another time he dragged me back into an hotel where we had been having a promotion celebration and taking two spoons and a cake-fork out of my handbag explained to the manager that his wife was a kleptomaniac.

But he could be crushing and scathing too. Like the time he wrote 'Darling Eejit Chuffie – You *can't* wear my old wings. Only anyone as dim as you would fail to be aware that the Barmaids' Union have adopted them as their badge. When the donor has left the woman his RAF friends can then see at a glance her accommodating nature.'

I could hear the snubbing voice as I read the words. There were times when I didn't know if he was joking.

What I did know was that he was my whole world. All the man I would ever want. I simply couldn't get enough of him.

—

At the office we started burning secret files, destroying dossiers, reports and maps. Sammy Koh had disappeared and taken various important documents with him. These documents included a map Morgan had given me to help me mark out important ports in the Dutch East Indies, and would be a real prize for the Japanese. All oil storage depots were marked on them. All airfields plainly marked.

Later in the morning the French Consul came to tell me that Sammy was in fact Japanese, had been spying for them for years, and was actually related to General Yamashito who took command of the invasion of Malaya.

The discovery of Sammy Koh's treachery upset me quite dreadfully. I found it hard to believe. How could a man who loved paintings, wild flowers and cats, and the poems of Gerald Manley Hopkins, be a scheming traitor?

How could I have been so stupid, so gullible? I should at least have been discerning enough to suspect his loyalty. I blamed myself entirely and set about preparing a long report making a clean breast of my guilt to the head of Postal Censorship. It took me hours to get the thing right and when at last I was satisfied I took my report and drove down to Collyer Quay.

I expected instant dismissal but my boss, I was told, had already left for Europe. There was no-one left to censor me.

Still no word from Sumatra. The daytime raids grew heavier and more frequent. Reports from the north were alarming. Then came the day when an officer I had never seen before, an Admin. man, appeared in the office and said I was to be evacuated.

Thinking this extraordinary as I had been told I was on the Free French Evacuation list, I asked who had sent him and he just showed me a signed piece of paper. It was good enough for me.

I asked where I was to be evacuated to and he said he was not allowed to divulge such information. He drove me to the hotel chalet. There was a hole in the roof over my bedroom and wood splinters everywhere. I was given five minutes to pack.

Cramming clothes, make-up, sponge-bag and Morgan's letters (for these were a must, although I hesitated momentarily) into a suitcase, I still had two minutes to spare. With that tingling sensation at the base of the spine, I grabbed a photograph of my grandfather, a half-sewn dress and a box of dates and said I was ready.

I slammed the door and all the glass fell out. The hotel cats sat in a row watching reproachfully.

'I don't suppose you have a car?' the tight-lipped Admin. man said.

'Yes, I do.'

'Then why didn't you say so,' he said irritably and tapped his foot as he watched me go over and get it out of the garage.

I was delighted I was to be allowed to take my car wherever I was going. It was my pride and joy, although Morgan didn't care for my taste. He thought it vulgar and unnecessary, but gave the game away when I asked him once what sort of girls attracted him. Off guard, he said, 'Lone girls driving sports cars really turn me on.'

Remembering all this, I dutifully followed the Admin. man in the jeep down through the town to the docks.

A red-faced warrant-officer with a gun motioned me to line my car up with two others at the edge of a jetty. An airman gave a wolf-whistle.

'Release the hand-brake,' someone called as I was about to get out. I did as I was told and got out and looked for the Admin. man. I could see him further down the quay and started to walk towards him. I was no more than twenty yards away from the car when I heard shots and turned. The crazy warrant-officer was shooting at the tyres of my beautiful car – bursting them. There was a lot of smoke and a horrible smell. I watched, speechless, scarcely believing my eyes as a gang of airmen began pushing the car over the edge of the dock into the backwater. They did the same with a Citroen and another car beside it.

I sank down on my case and began to cry for the first time since I was about fifteen and our parrot died.

The officer from the jeep jerked me to my feet muttering something about orders and scorched earth – and led me over to the other side of the quay and up the gangplank of a shabby looking ship about the size of a Channel boat. He explained tersely that pushing my car into the dock was to help jam up the depth available so that the entrance could not be used by the Japs.

Before it left the harbour, we heard aircraft overhead – someone said they were Navy Noughts. I was in a sort of stupor, quite unable to register the gravity of the situation. I heard bombs being dropped and strafing, and the sound of the aircraft going away.

When I got up and looked about it was to see that the ships on either side of us had been hit – the one aft had taken the brunt of the raid. Smoke was pouring from portholes – men were struggling out of them trying to hang on to ropes. Some were falling in the sea. Some of the godowns ashore had been hit and were blazing.

After some of the noise and vibrations had died down, we steamed out to sea. Out past the tiny islands so pretty in the pink sunset. The fishermen were still working on their nets.

I felt awful to be running away – leaving them to cope.

'I hope they think we are wounded or something,' I said to another Admin. officer leaning on the rail beside me. He was about to answer when an Army officer with a list advanced on us.

Pencil poised, he said, 'Flying-Officer Hardacre and wife – right? Now, has your wife brought any food?'

'She is not my wife and it doesn't look as if she has any food,' the man beside me snapped back.

The Army man consulted his list impatiently while I, feeling helpless and redundant, looked sadly on Singapore for the last time.

The man with the clip-board came back and told me somewhat curtly that it was Wing-Commander Morgan who had ordered me to be found and put on board.

THREE

It was a Dutch ship. I was shown to a cabin which I was to share with a very young Army wife with two babies, and a cabaret artist (married to an Army corporal). I had seen colourful sexy pictures of the singer-dancer outside a popular night spot in Singapore and was now quite cheered by her presence. She looked a lively character and was showing a fine disregard for the snobby Army wife's disapproval. She was on the floor cuddling one of the very plain, dribbling little brats, and its whines soon changed to cooings of delight. The silly Army bitch should have been grateful for I wasn't going to be any help.

I really didn't care for babies. I hated their sickening milky smell, their fragile pearly skins – the flesh creased as if tied with cotton – the freakish perfection of their tiny waving hands. It all bothered me.

Going back on deck and squatting on a packing case, I was presently joined by Flying-Officer Hardacre. He had managed to fill himself up with Bols gin from the smell of him, and set about showing me the less terse side of his personality. I much preferred the first impression.

He confided that we were going to Palembang in Sumatra, where Morgan was based, and I was so overjoyed at the news I sat and ate a scrappy meal of rice and doubtful prawns with him before going back to my cabin.

The babies (twins I supposed, although one was longer and thinner than the other) had been put to bed in my bunk. I didn't mind. I found a spare mattress in the corridor and dragged it in and lay down on the cabin floor and thought about Morgan and the bliss of seeing him. After a while I slept and dreamed of him until a baby roar snatched me back to reality.

During the rest of the short trip we saw no more enemy aircraft, but when we arrived at Palembang, we heard that the ship following us had been sunk during the night.

We arrived late in the afternoon and sat about for hours on our suitcases on deck waiting to be allowed to disembark. A great deal of arguing went on between the captain and the shore authorities.

At last, as it was beginning to get dark, some of us were allowed to go ashore and were taken in a small bus to the British HQ in the town.

Gradually all the women and children were collected by their husbands and taken off in various directions.

When Morgan appeared at long last, he looked tired and harassed and did not seem particularly pleased to see me. Almost the first thing he said, when I said something soppy about being together again, was 'Use your loaf! How long do you think we can last here?'

I thought he was being unduly pessimistic, which was out of character. I had already decided for myself that, now free of my former responsibilities, it would be marvellous to be able to devote my whole time to looking after him.

He had found a room for me in one of the hotels in the town. We went there and sat on the bed arguing and wrangling over the necessity for my leaving him yet again. There was no air-conditioning, the room swarmed with mosquitoes, and I felt dirty, bloody-minded and unloved. Instead of making him lie down and rest or comforting him – making the most of the precious time – I grew stubborn and petulant. At two o'clock a porter brought a message that he was wanted out at the airfield. He splashed his face with tepid water, squeezed me hard, promising to contact me as soon as possible the next day, and left.

It was the hottest, longest night I ever remember. I dozed fitfully for a couple of hours then got up and had a bath and went to find some breakfast. After mooning about the hotel for a while

I craved some fresh air and left a message at the desk to say I would be back in an hour, and went out.

In the main street I saw a group of Dutch women clustered round what I made out to be a sort of Citizens' Advice bureau and went and joined them. One of them spoke good English. She told me that there was no hope of any more transport out of the island by sea. They were the very last to get passages on a ship leaving in two hours for India. She asked me where I was staying and if my husband was in Palembang. I told her, and she said there was no need to use the hotel which was not very sympathetic – there were lots of lovely little houses abandoned by Dutch couples.

She called over the heads of her friends to a fat-faced young man to confirm all this. In reply, he handed me a bunch of keys and a piece of paper with an address on it and told me to help myself.

Back at the hotel there was still no word from Morgan. I took a taxi and gave the paper to the dark-skinned driver and told him to take me there.

It was a charming little house on the fringe of the town, with flame of the forest trees in the garden and porta-laca flowers bordering the path to the door.

The owners must have left in a great hurry for the drawers in the bedroom were half full of clothes, there were toothbrushes in the bathroom, and a half-finished piece of embroidery lay on a sofa in the sitting-room as if momentarily cast aside.

A very young Javanese servant, a boy hardly more than a child in clean white drill jacket and pants appeared, looking scared, from the back of the house. He confirmed in pidgin English that Sahib and Memsahib had gone away and asked if I were the new Mem. I said, perhaps, in Malay, and perhaps I should come back. He seemed pleased and started straightening the chairs and flicking at imaginary dust.

The house was small and simply but tastefully furnished, the plumbing primitive but adequate. I gave the boy some money and told him to buy bread and milk and coffee and that I would come back later.

Back at the hotel, there was still no news from Morgan. I lay on the bed and slept with one eye open, for hours, in the stuffy narrow room. At about seven o'clock Morgan came in. Without giving him a chance to speak I started blurting out the bit about there being no more transport out of the island and how I had found a perfect little house and begged him to let us go there right away.

He looked wearier than ever. The skin seemed drawn tight over his cheek-bones and his eyes were pink-rimmed with fatigue.

He didn't say anything, just looked around the dreadful room, sighed and smiled a benign smile and said that if that was what I really wanted, we would do that thing.

On the way, he told me that I was to be put on an aircraft leaving at six-thirty the following morning. As soon as we got to the little house, he lay down on the bed and just passed out. He was snoring before I could drag any of his clothes off. I lay down close beside him and wept. The mosquitoes were even worse than at the hotel and it was just as hot.

The Javanese boy called us as I had told him to do, at five o'clock, bringing us some syrupy lukewarm coffee and currant buns.

Morgan apologised for his loutish behaviour in falling asleep and told me that he hadn't slept on a bed for almost a week. Then, in very few words, he told me just how grim the situation really was. I didn't ask any more questions. We made a solemn promise that eventually we would try to meet in Ceylon, at the Galle Face Hotel in Colombo. That was where most of the evacuee ships were going from Batavia and it was to Batavia (in Java, and now known as Jakarta) that I was being flown.

At six we left the little house and anxious-to-please child-servant and drove out to the airfield. None of the Blenheims was to be seen. It looked a sinister place, just a patch hewn out of the evil green jungle.

Two old Lockheed-Hudsons were lined up to take twenty or so women, a few children and luggage. There was more of the inevitable hanging about and Morgan kept being called away from me to answer a telephone. The Dutch women looked a moronic lot.

Suddenly, everything was declared ready and there was no time to say any of the things we had to say to each other.

Morgan introduced me to the pilot of the plane I was to board, a giant Dutchman with hands like hams wearing a green jacket with the KLM insignia on the lapels. Morgan said he was now officially in the Dutch Air Force, but this was obviously a joke. I tried to laugh but Morgan had my face between his hands and was saying 'All right? The Galle Face. See you.' Then I was inside the plane looking down on him. Before the aircraft wheeled round, I caught my last glimpse of him taking off his flat hat to mop his forehead, exaggerating his relief for the benefit of the ground crews.

I was full of foreboding, unshed tears and a terrible awareness of the evil aspect of this particular airfield. As if to underline my suspicions, I noticed a gigantic, strange four-engined bomber which had crash-landed and turned over. Like a mythical outsize bird with a broken back. It was the first Flying Fortress I had ever seen.

FOUR

When we had swung into position for take-off, the pilot produced a tin of ginger biscuits and sent his radio-operator to offer me one. After a while he called me forward to sit near him and started to tell me about himself. He came from Amsterdam where his father was an undertaker. I should go to Holland. It was the best place in the world.

He was a good pilot. After about forty minutes flying we were spotted by an enemy aircraft which circled and followed us. The Dutchman told me to go back to my own seat and fasten myself in tightly. We would have some fun.

He started to do some clever weaving, treating the aircraft as if it were a small light thing, in and out of the clouds, climbing then falling until we were skimming the white foam of the waves. We lost our pursuer and finished the journey almost at sea-level along the coast of Java.

I don't think the other passengers had been aware of the menacing Jap. They were mostly middle-aged and drab, and some of them looked ill as well as indifferent.

At Batavia airport we were shepherded into a transit office and I met up again with the young English Army wife from the ship, with her babies and Nana, the dancer. They had been at the airport hotel for two days waiting for a plane and had just been told there was no hope of one for the time being.

We three and the babies were then separated from the rest and taken along to a bay marked 'Aliens' and told to wait.

The babies looked quite cheerful and more attractive than the last time I had seen them, but their mother was still sniffling and complaining, and seemed more concerned with the lumpy basket containing bottles, tins and nappies than with the babies themselves. She was also, I noticed, keeping Nana in her place.

I couldn't understand the cabaret girl's interest in the tiresome children, feeling that it was a stupid self-indulgence for anyone to produce babies at times like these, when I caught a certain expression on the full-lipped dusky face. There was no doubt about it. I looked down at her belly. It pushed out against her tight, light silk skirt. She was, of course, pregnant herself.

After our papers had been inspected we were all herded back with the Dutch women and into a bus. An official told us we were being taken, just for the night, to stay at a house outside the town.

We drove for miles, leaving the town far behind. After about two hours we slowed down and turned in at a pair of great gates in a high wall with barbed wire running along the top. In a flash, I knew about the place. A huge reformatory type of establishment used by the Dutch for housing doubtful characters while decisions were made.

It was the Tjitrap camp. A camp used for interning the Germans and Vichyists rounded up in the Netherlands East Indies. I knew quite a lot about the place through my job. I had in fact been directly responsible for putting people inside.

Hoist with my own petard, I thought, as the gates clanged shut and were chained behind us. How Morgan would love this.

The gate-keeper and the attendants would recognise no difference whatsoever between us and suspect Nazis. The administration wouldn't change like magic for us. I knew what we would find before we reached the house itself.

Not one of the Dutch women protested. I looked closely at the one sitting next to me. Her face was twitchy, and saliva ran from one corner of her mouth. Another woman near the front of the bus was singing faintly in a high-pitched tuneless voice. Then I inspected each one of them in turn and the dreaded truth struck me. They were all abnormal.

'Didn't you know? Nut-cases,' Nana said, watching me in amusement. 'They are all harmless. Rather sweet, some of them,' she added. 'Come from a sanatorium in Medan. It was bombed.'

A belt of high trees encircled the place. When the bus stopped the silence was loud.

I felt claustrophobic, completely cut-off from the outside world.

Nana put her hand on mine and said 'It won't be too bad, I expect.'

I clasped the outstretched hand and smiled at her. She was a nice girl and I was glad she was there.

At least I knew that the Dutch authorities had brought us here because they simply didn't know what the Hell to do with us.

FIVE

We trooped into a big hall, bare except for long trestle tables and benches. The only light came from a few small paraffin lamps.

If there were no more planes, we could be here for the duration of the war. The sooner they handed us over to the Japs the better. Anything would be better than this mad Sartre-like ambience.

We were shown beds in cells. Narrow little wooden frames with wafer-thin mattresses. A yard behind had stone troughs for washing and holes in concrete latrines behind flimsy barriers.

A huge woman built like a door came to tell us there would be a meal at six o'clock when a bell would be rung.

When it sounded, I put my hands over my ears for it sounded like the funeral bell in the village at home.

We were given plates of gritty bean soup, bread, jam and tea. There was also some soft yellow substance which looked like butter and may have been margarine but had absolutely no taste at all.

An older woman in a brown uniform, presumably the Matron, appeared and said some prayers over us, then with two other hatchet-faced females in aprons, walked round inspecting us — treating us all like amiable lunatics. When we asked questions they smiled mechanically, nodded patiently, folded their arms and went away.

It was like a bad dream. Anything would be better.

The Dutch authorities for all I knew, having more or less finished their evacuation schemes, had simply taken us out of the mainstream and shelved us. It was possible there were plans to ship us all somewhere *en masse* or, and this was the thought that nagged most at the back of my mind, they might conveniently forget about us.

Most of the Dutch women by this time had become resigned to the conditions and gone to bed. Brenda, the Army wife, had curled up and cried herself to sleep leaving Nana to cope with the babes. The mosquitoes made it impossible to sit near a lamp, so I just walked up and down.

When it was quite dark I slipped round the back of the yard and down the drive to try to find the man at the gate. I came to the lodge without any difficulty and knocked on the door. The big Matron opened the door.

I said firmly that I wished to use the telephone. She said, no telephone, but I pointed to the wires and pushed past her into the room. There was a good bright light in there. I opened my purse and showed her a fifty-guilder note.

She led me through to another room where three or four people were talking and drinking round a table and then on into a smaller room where there was a telephone on the wall and a pile of directories in a bookcase.

I hadn't the faintest idea what to look for so flicked through the pages for inspiration. A place name leapt to my notice. Buitenzorg. I knew a man who came from there. An American. We had met him at a party in Singapore. He had said, if ever we were in Java, to be sure and look him up. Now was the time, but what was his name? Ross – no – Gus, that was it. Gus Headley. Clever girl. I looked under the aitches. Headley, G.H., Buitenzorg 436.

Lifting the receiver I asked for the number in French then in English. The operator understood and asked what number I was calling from. I gave it to her and within seconds another voice came on the line.

'Mr Headley's house?'

'Ya – Ya. Yes. Is Mr Headley house here. Mr Headley he go out. Coming back night time. I give message OK.'

'You tell Mr Headley – Mrs Morgan from Singapore. Telephone Batavia 14. Goodbye. Thank you.'

I gave the money to the waiting woman and indicated that the telephone would ring for me and she must call me when it did. I fingered other money in my purse. She understood perfectly.

Running back to the house, I felt elated. Freedom was more important than safety.

The call came through at seven the next morning. It was a miracle. Gus Headley remembered me, was delighted, flattered and verbose. He arrived in person within the hour in a magnificent Cadillac and swept me off without explanation or hindrance.

SIX

Bowling along in the well-sprung car, I told Gus Headley all that had happened and that I thought it best to try to get to Bandoeng where I knew there was an RAF HQ. I could get a job with them for they sometimes took on civilian staff. Then I should be able to keep in touch with Morgan or at least get news of his squadron.

Gus patted my knee, then seized my hand and said that if things got much worse he would be leaving for the States – he didn't say how – and that I would be very welcome to go along with him if I cared to. He grinned and looked at me in a meaningful way as he said this, and I withdrew my fingers, blushed, and pointed to a group of workers in the paddy-fields saying something inane about their hats.

His house was enormous, cool, and expensively furnished. It was opulent and overdone, very self-consciously oriental in a *House and Garden* manner. In my frame of mind I loved all the manifestations of wealth. The plumbing was fantastic.

I lay for a long time in scented water in a sunken turquoise bath-tub in an air-conditioned bathroom, deciding to relax and deal with each new situation as it presented itself. Fate was momentarily on my side.

For lunch we ate avocado pears from the garden and a golden *pilau* with giant fried prawns and bits of tangy raw ham. Before we got to the pudding course I had made up my mind that Gus was one of the kindest men I had ever met. He was certainly the cleanest. His shirt, which he probably changed several times a day, was immaculate. His soft foulard tie was the same shade of pale terracotta as his socks, and toned perfectly with the sand-coloured Palm Beach suiting. Everything was initialled – his shirt, cuff-links, handkerchief. What if he did look like an advert from *Men's Wear Daily*. I liked it. He smelled clean too – of some costly cologne, a mixture of lavender and leather.

Up till now I had always agreed with Morgan that any sort of cosmetic for men was effete and sissy and simply not to be tolerated. Now I was all for it.

Gus had to go back to the office for a while after the meal and suggested I should take a nap and meet him again for drinks about six. This was the life of the glossy magazines. I liked it.

I wandered about the terrace and water-garden for a while in spite of the intense heat and humidity, and then took another bath just for the hell of it.

In my suitcase I had a jade patterned silk dress and a matching string of beads. Pulling the dress out I gave it a good shaking and hung it up to steam. Miraculously the crushed look disappeared. Drying myself in a huge purple bath sheet, I helped myself liberally to body lotion and powder from the well-stocked glass shelf and tried brushing my hair a new shape – gently forward over the brow and sleekly back behind the ears. I really should make an effort to look good. A vivid lipstick and lots of vaseline on my eyelids made me look sophisticated. I tried on the dress and the swinging beads and watched myself mincing towards the mirror. I looked like one of those Miss World contestants, advancing on the interviewer. 'I just want to travel and be happy,' I mouthed, pouted, and collapsed onto the low bed giggling like a schoolgirl.

Recalling the American's expression in the car that morning when he had suggested I should go to the States with him, I stopped laughing and began to wonder what in fact he might expect of me.

Just then, a noise from the courtyard rivetted my attention. A door in the wall closed and I saw a Javanese girl of exceptional beauty tripping across the flagstones. She was perfect – a living statuette. She was wearing a white lace *kebaya* (a short tight-fitting blouse leaving the golden brown midriff bare) and an even tighter sarong, embroidered in scarlet and orange. Diamonds glinted on the lobes of her ears with that unmistakeable brilliance which confirms the real thing and she had eyelashes like palm-fronds, also genuine.

In one hand she carried a scarf and a small wicker basket. Her toe nails were painted vermilion. She knocked at the door in the far corner and a servant let her in. I heard distant tinkling laughter, more light tapping footsteps, a door closing, then silence.

The oriental girl was no servant. Did Gus intend to keep her concealed or should we be three for dinner?

In either case, her presence surely cleared up any doubts I had been harbouring. I took off the slinky green dress and stowed it back into the case and rang a bell. When the boy came, I asked if he could get my white dress – the one in which I had arrived, pressed before dinner. He said, the *amah* would wash and press it very well within about two hours.

I lay across the bed and thought of Morgan and whether he would disapprove of my being where I was. I would go to Bandoeng and perhaps I would see him soon. I slept without dreaming until the boy came knocking on the door with my dress freshly laundered and carefully ironed. He also brought me a glass of lemon tea on a tiny enamelled tray.

Almost the first thing Gus said when I went to join him just after six, was, 'I find I have some of my staff coming for a poker game this evening.'

He hoped I wouldn't be concerned for my reputation, but if being found alone in the house with him worried me, there was another solution. He had a small chalet up in the mountains, just off the road to Bandoeng. I could go and spend the night up there and be taken on to Bandoeng the next day.

I quickly accepted the suggestion and after a drink with him went off to collect my things. My ego a bit deflated, I had enough sense to realise this was an easy way out of what could have been a very tricky situation. There was no poker game arranged. The beautiful Javanese girl I had seen arriving, had come to spend the night and he had somehow to get me out of the house. The car and driver were waiting.

Gus came and wished me goodbye and told me he had booked a room for me in an hotel in Bandoeng. I must be sure and keep in touch with him and that the trip to the States could still be arranged. He offered me money but I assured him I had enough. He gave me one of his business cards and waved us off.

We began to climb as soon as we left the house and night fell like a curtain so that I could see nothing of the landscape. It grew rapidly colder and I could hear waterfalls and little streams as we climbed mile after mile on rough roads before reaching the chalet.

When I got out of the car I could feel misty rain on my face and see twinkling lights like a handful of jewels far far below on the flat dark plain.

Very deftly the Javanese boy, Rafi, moved about the tiny house. He lit lamps, drew curtains, making the place instantly bright and welcoming. There was even a small radio which he switched on to produce repetitive *ronggeng* music, moaning on and on with no beginning and no end. A fire of knobbly twigs began to splutter and flare in the open grate. I tried speaking Malay to Rafi, but he did not understand. English was no good either, so I had to make do with miming and smiles. He was so efficient and resourceful, speech wasn't really necessary.

Showing me the bedroom and bathroom he pointed to the taps, looking happy over the first, blowing on his hands and shaking his head and shivering over the other in an effort to show me how the tiny geyser worked.

I read part of a Thornton Wilder novel for a while, one of a complete collection in the bookcase. It was a novelty feeling cold and enjoying the leaping flames. In no time Rafi was back with soup in a pretty rice bowl on a tray. After a while he brought a delicious omelette, *chapati*, and some of the round soft white fruit with thick purple skin called mangosteens.

Before going to bed, I carried the tray out to the kitchen and managed to convey how much I had enjoyed the food and by drawing a large clock face on a writing pad that I would like to start off for Bandoeng at eight o'clock the next morning.

Rafi grinned and nodded his understanding.

I stepped onto the terrace and looked out into the night. So much had happened in the two days since I had left Morgan, and I was about to go even further away from him. A cold wind nibbled at me. Another cold wind nibbled away inside. What was to become of me?

Getting undressed quickly, I snuggled under the blankets and tried not to think about being alone, perched up a mountain in an uncanny coldness. After a while I slept, and dreamed I was in my first boarding school.

Dressing the following morning, I was so cold I put on all the clothes I had with me except the silk dress.

Setting off down the mountain I saw that we were above the cloud line. We wound down and down the spiral road and I saw that each little ledge or plateau was fertile and cultivated with infinite care. The wet rice-fields looked like a large-scale rock garden, and the patchwork of vegetation was the greenest and most lush I had ever seen in the East.

Here and there we passed groups of workers. They all paused, smiled and waved. Some of them were beautiful with their flat high-cheek-boned faces and wide straw hats. Some carried yokes with swinging pails of water. Their colouring was darker than the Malays, the features stronger, and I thought they looked happier.

Near the road and outside the rattan and mud houses flowers grew in masses of orange pink and flame, kembang sphati and flamboyant. On the skyline to the east I could see the sinister shapes of volcanic mountains.

There was something strange about the light, the colours were so bright they hurt the eyes, and once I glimpsed a green jungle fowl swooping out of a clump of bamboo. I had never in all my life seen such luxuriance of plant life, such a richness of flowers. I remembered Gus telling me that it rained for a longish period every day so that plant growth went on at all seasons of the year.

As we lost height, I began peeling off clothes, jacket, two sweaters then finally down to the sleeveless dress.

For several miles we crossed a plain and after about an hour began to climb again.

*

Bandoeng, situated on a high plateau in the middle of the island of Java, was considered a resort town in peace time, and was full of luxury hotels and bars. It is quite high above sea level but not as high as the mountain range of the previous night. We drove down a wide main street with concrete buildings and many modern hotels of varied architecture predominating. A sort of oriental Harrogate. We passed one hotel which had an impressive fountain playing and behind, a semi-circular terrace where people sat drinking. There were sounds of western Palm Court music from within the building, and smartly clad waiters and bell-boys flitted about. It was modestly called the Savoy, and was the one in which Gus had booked me a room.

A porter came as soon as we drew up and took my bag. I thanked Rafi as well as I was able, gave him money to get himself some food, scribbled a note for Gus and sent the boy on his way.

I recognised two Air Force wives as soon as I went into the foyer. They greeted me with some interest and surprise, told me they were waiting for a car to take them to board a ship in Batavia, then turned their backs on me and continued their own blood-stained gossip.

After I had registered, unpacked and had a sandwich in my room, I took a taxi to RAF Headquarters. The taxi broke down and by the time the driver had managed to get it going again, everybody at HQ was packing up work for the day. I couldn't find anyone I knew. A sergeant in the front office suggested I should come back the next day. I could easily get a lift from the Savoy, he said, as most of the personnel were staying there.

Feeling that I couldn't bear to see anyone until I had some news of Morgan, or at least until I had established and justified my right to be in the place, I put on my dark glasses and avoided people in the lobby.

A Dutch girl working in Reception said the wives I had seen earlier had now left and others were going off to Sourabaja within the next few days. She also told me that news from Sumatra was bad. The Japanese had established a stronghold in the north of the island. Morgan was bound to be coming south before long. I had to hang on and see him.

Bed seemed my best refuge. The fatigue of the last few days was catching up on me. I locked my door and slept till daylight. By seven I was ready and waiting to cadge a lift from anyone in RAF uniform I happened to see in the foyer.

SEVEN

I sought out the Personnel officer who turned out to be a timid squadron-leader with hay fever. Expecting to be rebuked by someone for having left the camp at Batavia, I was relieved to find no-one knew anything about it or me. The Personnel man assured me that my bill would be paid at the hotel and that, if I wished, a job would be found for me right away. There was no other news from Sumatra.

After sniffing something from a syringe-shaped instrument up each nostril in turn, the squadron-leader sent me along to a Group-Captain Ryan who, he said, needed a secretary.

The name didn't mean anything to me, but he turned out to be the husband of one of the women I had encountered on arriving. He was the weak silent type, more brass than brains I thought privately, and in all fairness told him my typing wasn't much good and my filing even worse.

For some reason, he thought this very funny and asked me if I would have dinner with him that evening. I said thank you, that would be nice, but could I please start to work right away.

With a half-smile he dictated two letters to London. One, a complaint about a batch of airmen who had arrived without the correct inoculations, and another asking for filing cabinets:

This took me about an hour and for the rest of the morning until lunch, I busied myself writing a long screed to Morgan with illustrations. It turned out to be the only letter he ever received from me in Dutch territory.

Lunching in the canteen, I chatted to some of the cipher clerks. News from Palembang was gloomy. Parachutists had taken the important spots on the north-east coast and wrecked fuel supplies. Similar attacks were expected sooner or later all over Sumatra.

I asked tentatively about the wives in the hotel and the ship from Sourabaja, and was told that no-one who was not already listed could hope for a place. The next possibility was another American tanker coming into Batavia.

On my way back to my office, I spotted rows of small steel filing cabinets in an alcove. They were all empty. I got a passing airman to help me move one into my office and started filing all the papers and letters I could lay my hands on.

The group-captain's indulgent smile did little to reassure me. It was apparent that he had no work to do himself and spent his time telephoning his friends, smoking like a chimney, or just picking his nose.

Aware that anything I did was unavailing and pointless, it was comforting to be near the radio-room and better than sitting in the hotel bar.

The enemy was advancing now at such a rate, it would not be long before the business of destroying documents began, just as I had done in Singapore.

I dined at my boss's table that evening and every evening. He was really very nice and at first rather shy. He seemed to take it for granted that he was my protector outside office hours and as he had such gallant manners and a certain authority, I would have been stupid and churlish to sit in my room alone.

It was far better to go with the crowd and pick up what scraps of information I could.

The 'grouper' went on for hours about his life and times in India and his dog days at Cranwell. It was all very boring and interlaced with turn of the century phrases.

There were times when I wished fervently that I had made more friends among Service people in Malaya. I had been so engrossed in my own work and otherwise totally preoccupied with Morgan, that I had never felt the need for other people. Even so, it was comforting to encounter people, however slight the acquaintance in Singapore, and I used to find myself glad to see any of them who turned up at the hotel.

Occasionally over the radio, interspersing the usual *joget* (modern Malay dance music), we would hear 'Land of Hope and Glory' booming out. I had always disliked the song, finding its sentiment embarrassing. Someone said Singapore played it every hour.

There was a party every night now. Everyone drank too much and then went on to a sleazy club across the street or to a dimly lit nightclub some five miles out of town called the Black Cat. The place was small, upholstered in traditional red plush and gilt, and always packed to suffocation. Its main attraction was a very fat albino pianist who spoke a smattering of most European languages and played like Fats Waller.

Rows broke out frequently between the Australians and Dutch soldiers who seemed to hate each other's guts.

Unfortunately when the group-captain had had a certain amount to drink he always wanted to dance and not content with just ambling round, it had to be 'cheek to cheek'. There was nothing for me to do but submit and try to look as if I was enjoying it.

From time to time he would disappear ostensibly to telephone, and on return would reward me with a titbit of news of Morgan's squadron. Sometimes the news was stale or 'duff gen', or if he was very drunk it might be something I had already told him, earlier.

I began to suspect that he had a weak bladder and that he made up these snippets in the loo.

One evening however, an airman on a motor-bike arrived with a copy of a cable addressed to me, so I hastily took back a lot of my uncharitable thoughts as I opened it and read:

EIGHT HUNDRED GUILDERS YOUR NAME DE
JAVESCHE BANK STP
POOR CHUFF NO SARONGS AT ALL LOVE M.

Morgan was alive and well and still clowning and I was rich. I wept with excitement and joy, and the group-captain lent me his handkerchief.

I bought myself a dress made of fine cotton batik with

flame-coloured flowers all over it because its colour was typical of the island, some sandals and a blue silk scarf.

A few days after the shopping spree I began to notice there were fewer and fewer people about the hotel. That evening, a Naval officer to whom I had never spoken, approached me, invited me to have a drink with him and in the most grave and fatherly manner advised me to make whatever plans I could to leave the island. I assured him that I would do exactly as I was told if the RAF suggested evacuation.

Even as we were chatting, an air-raid warning sounded. The siren for the area was on the roof of the hotel and the din was ear-splitting. We dutifully hurried down to the shelters. There, I confided in him that I felt this terrible need to see Morgan once more, that without him I could see no life for myself. The grey-haired man said Morgan was a lucky man but made me promise I would get away as soon as possible.

EIGHT

Up to date the raids had not done much damage in the town, but the airfield had suffered badly.

I woke up in the early hours one morning with a headache and a nagging presentiment that something was very wrong. At breakfast, over the radio, I heard that Palembang had fallen. A colossal parachutist attack. Some of our aircraft had got away but no further details were available.

The horror of the next three or four days was nightmarish. The biggest dread of all was that I might be snatched up and sent away without knowing what had happened to Morgan.

On the morning of the fourth day, I was waiting in the hall for the group-captain, when a dispatch-rider came to the desk. A name was called and suddenly everyone was looking at me. I opened the pink paper and read the typewritten words:

HUSBAND WOUNDED HOSPITAL BATAVIA.

No clue from where it had been sent, no name of sender. It didn't matter, I had to go to Batavia at once.

There was only one man on duty at the reception desk and he was already answering two telephones and coping with a lot of querulous Dutchmen.

I looked around desperately and saw a young man I knew slightly, called Kurt Van de Laan. He was half-Dutch and half-French and worked for the local airline. He was very attractive and had the Frenchman's way of flirting with every woman as if she expected it. I had met him first at a dinner-party in Kuala Lumpar and was flattered by his interest in me. Now was the moment to find whether this was genuine.

Seizing his arm I said 'Will you help me?' He turned and took both my hands and looked into my eyes with his curious lion-coloured ones. He looked younger and fairer than I remembered him in uniform. I showed him the cable and he said, 'Leave it to me, dah-leeng. I will arrange everything.'

He said that he would go back to the airfield, get me a seat on the next plane – they were still operating two a day – and that I should pack a case and stay in my room until he rang.

Forty minutes later, I was on my way. He saw me onto the small plane and gave me the names of four hospitals in Batavia, headed by the military one. He also added the name of a colleague at the airport in case I needed help finding accommodation.

Within the next hour I was in Batavia, hailing a taxi – choosing a driver wearing a *songkok*, the black velvet, flower-pot shaped hat worn by most Malays. I was lucky, for the man did speak some Malay, and took me quickly to the Military Hospital. There, I wrote 'Wing-Commander MORGAN' on a sheet of foolscap paper and showed it to a clerk in an office near the main entrance. The man consulted a ledger, shook his head and in halting English told me that the casualties from Palembang had not yet been listed. It was possible my husband was in the hospital somewhere – there were many wounded. I could look for myself.

Inside were scenes of unbelievable carnage. The place was overflowing with bodies. Not all of them had beds. Some lay on strips of canvas on the floor.

I searched the faces, trying not to look at the bodies. Some had very little clothing, only bandages soaked with blood. Everywhere the smell of unwashed humanity mingled with the odour of ether and urine. Flies buzzed and crawled in their hundreds.

After almost an hour I knew that it was hopeless to search further. The overworked nurses cast irritable glances at me. One pushed me roughly out of her way. I didn't resent their attitude. It was a hopeless situation and I was a damned nuisance.

I went back to the clerk at the office and he gave me the names of several schools turned into temporary hospitals. Morgan was not in any of them nor in the other hospitals on Kurt's list.

NINE

Defeated and disconsolate I asked the taxi-driver to take me back to the first hospital but he too had had enough and refused to go further. I offered him money, much more than his due, and he livened up immediately and drove off. At the hospital, I told him I didn't need him any more, but now he knew that I had plenty of money he made it clear he was happy to wait indefinitely.

The clerk came round the counter towards me this time, waving the piece of paper with Morgan's name on it. Morgan had been there all the time, he said, in the operating theatre. Now it was over. I could see him for a few minutes only.

He had been put in a tiny room to himself, a sort of cubicle at the end of a long ward on the ground floor. From this fact alone, I knew that he must be very ill.

At first I thought he was unconscious. He lay with his eyes closed and his legs in massive plaster casts propped higher than his body. The lower half of his face was painted with gentian-violet and his fair curly hair – the only recognisable bit of him, was badly singed.

There was a horrible smell in the room, putrid and pungent, which I couldn't identify. I stood quite still by the bed for a few minutes and saw his eyelids flicker. To know that he was alive was for the moment, enough. I waited and watched and presently he opened his eyes and looked at me but there was no hint of recognition. The third time he opened his eyes I put my head close to his face. The eyes were still vacant but he raised a hand towards me and tried to grin. The next instant his whole expression hardened – the muscles of his sunken cheeks twitched and beads of sweat stood out on his forehead. I mopped his brow gently with my scarf and he made small grunting noises then closed his eyes again and lay still.

A nurse came in and said I must leave, but that I could come back the next day. She looked closely at Morgan, took his pulse, said he was sleeping now and that was good. Tomorrow, she said, he would be a little better.

I managed after a lot of waiting about, to find one of the surgeons who had operated on him. A tall thin Dutchman who looked worn out but who was gentle and patient with me. He explained in limited English that my husband's legs were full of holes and lumps of cordite. The wounds were badly gangrenous but they might manage to save one of the limbs. At least that is what I understood him to mean. He added that the crucial point would come in about one week's time. He was also very weak through loss of blood.

Apologising for keeping him, I asked hurriedly if he thought it possible to get my husband transferred to the hospital in Bandoeng where he would have better nursing in a better climate. He promised to see what could be done about this – he would let me know – perhaps tomorrow.

All the time he was speaking with me he was looking at his watch and edging away towards the door. I dared not keep him a moment longer from all those others who urgently needed his skill.

I managed to get a room at the Hotel des Indes. Then I went to the medical unit at RAF HQ. I had been told the CO was a group-captain but I didn't know his name. I was told he was not available. A very young flight-lieutenant offered to help me. He had Morgan's name on a list, with injuries listed as 'facial and arms'. I corrected this and asked about possibilities of a move to Bandoeng. The flight-lieutenant said he would make a note of my request but that he could do nothing until the CO came back.

Wearily I went back to the hotel. The first person I saw as I passed the bar was a group-captain with the familiar medical insignia. He must be the senior doctor. He was with a blonde woman and they were laughing with their heads close together.

Whatever they were discussing was remote from war. Resisting the temptation to walk straight up to him and confront him with my problem, I went off to my room and straight to bed.

The next morning I went down to HQ early and sat for three hours in the corridor until the group-captain came in. After about ten minutes I was allowed in to see him. He seemed to have difficulty in focussing and looked as if he had a hangover.

I had to begin all over again, and state my case and plea from the beginning. As I was asking about Bandoeng another officer came in with a quite different list from the one I had been shown the day before. Morgan's name was on it and his injuries listed as 'legs – possible amputation – and head injuries'.

The group-captain said he was already considering transferring some cases to Bandoeng and he was expecting to discuss this with doctors at the Military Hospital.

I asked next what possibility there was for a hospital ship. He said, practically nil, but in the event of one turning up, he would see that Morgan's name was on the list. I left my room number and the hotel telephone number with him and he promised to get in touch if Morgan was to be moved.

'And a place on the ship?' I persisted.

'Possible but unlikely,' was all he would say.

There were various people I knew by sight about the hotel but I wasn't in the mood for talking to anyone and sat in my room until it was time to go to the hospital.

On the way I bought some fruit, cigarettes and a bottle of expensive eau-de-cologne.

TEN

Morgan was propped in an uncomfortable-looking position, but definitely 'sitting-up' and I was amazed at how much better he looked. I avoided looking at his legs, and went over and put my arms very gently round him. It didn't take me long to realise that the appalling smell came from him. He kissed me, winced with pain and ridiculed me about my long face and sour expression.

'Cheer up, love,' he said. 'It'll take more than this to flatten me. I hope to God you've brought me a drink.'

I showed him the fruit and cigarettes and splashed some of the costly cologne around. It had about as much effect as a lavender bag in a fish-market.

I had to get out of the room, afraid I should be sick, and made the request for a drink my excuse. I found a nurse and she showed me where to find glasses and a tap. I asked her about the smell and she told me it was the smell of gangrene but that it was better to pretend to my husband that the smell came from the river. I took a sip of water myself, felt better and hurried back.

'Use your loaf, darling – I need a real drink. Bring me some whisky, for Christ's sake – '

'Have you asked the doctor if it's all right?' I ventured.

'Huff the medicos – be a good girl and do as I say. Now, listen. I am trying to get a transfer to Bandoeng in a few days. I might be able to get permission to take you along on the train with me. I gather there's more room and it's not so stinking hot up there, so stay near a telephone. Where are you anyway – at that great gin palace, the des Indes, I suppose. Who's there? Anyone I know?'

Morgan was in command again. He was going to be all right, I thought, but even as I thought this, I noticed a lot of blood welling through the plaster around the ankle of his right leg and went out to ask the nurse about it. She said that was the leg they might have to amputate, and that there was nothing more to be done for the time being. He was due to have a tranfusion later in the day.

When I got back to the room, he looked much paler and seemed to have dropped off to sleep. I sat watching him for about an hour until the nurse came back and told me it was time for me to go. I asked her about the whisky and she said it was strictly against the rules and would be very bad for him.

The next day he didn't wake at all while I was there. The nurse explained that he had had a very bad night after the tranfusion and they had now put him under sedation.

I didn't manage to speak to him again until after the call for me came from HQ and we were both on the train to Bandoeng. I had filled in part of the waiting time by writing to Morgan's mother and to my parents. I posted the letters hopefully in the main post office but of course they never reached their destination.

At the station waiting for the ambulance to arrive from the hospital, I met up with a flight-sergeant from Morgan's Squadron who was touchingly glad to see me. He was able to tell me roughly what had happened at Palembang.

The Japs had launched their biggest parachute attack to date. The few remaining serviceable aircraft managed to get away. The Australians defending the base with all its stores and spares and fuel supplies ran off into the jungle. Morgan and an airman were trying to man one of the two Bofors guns on the perimeter, when a shell exploded in the breach. The airman was killed outright. Morgan was blown several yards and later picked up and thrown on a coal truck with other wounded and driven down to the port.

Not until he reached the coast of Java three days later did he have any treatment for his wounds. All his clothing had been blown off in the explosion except for the webbing belt of a revolver holster.

It was at this point in the story, I heard Morgan's own voice as they were trying to haul his stretcher out of the ambulance. I kept out of the way until they had him and all the other stretcher cases safely on the train, then I asked a young Army doctor if I might go and see him. He said yes, of course, but I must be careful not to block the gangway between the bunks as the two nurses needed to move freely – they had some very ill people to look after.

Morgan was really pleased to see me and offered me a drink from the bottle he had on his chest. he looked flushed and smelled strongly of whisky, but it was marvellous to hear him sounding his old belligerent self again. He introduced me to a very young Army officer who looked all of eighteen and had just had his right arm amputated. he was doing a crossword puzzle in an old copy of *The Times*, and was getting no help at all from Morgan.

I had to go and find my own seat further down the train soon after this so didn't see Morgan again until he was being carried off at Bandoeng station. His face was drawn and pallid now above the grotesque purple chin and I could see by the wet forehead that he must be suffering dreadfully.

The jolting of the train had caused his wounds to open, for there was a lot of blood soaking through the edges of the plaster and making a pool under his feet.

The nurses waiting at the hospital in Bandoeng had frozen jug-like faces, and they barred me from going in. I may be admitted, one told me, to visit my husband between eleven and twelve the next day. I asked if he might be given something to ease his pain and was told that that was a matter for professional decision.

ELEVEN

I walked the two miles or so back to the Savoy slowly to kill time.

Crossing the hotel foyer, it struck me that there was something odd about the place. The lights were dimmer, there was no-one at all on duty at the desk, and very few people about anywhere.

Taking my key from its pigeon-hole, I hurried to my room which was on the ground floor across a courtyard.

The door stood open which was puzzling. The room was empty. That is, empty of anything familiar or personal. No brushes on the dressing table, no books or papers to be seen.

Frantically, I began pulling out drawers, opening cupboards. I stood still, laughing at myself. Morgan was right, I really was a fool. I was in the wrong room.

Going out into the corridor, I looked closely at the number on the door. I had not made a mistake. It was my room all right, but someone had removed all my things.

It was like one of those dreams when you find yourself naked in public.

I ran to the manager's office. There was no need for me to say anything. He was horrified to see me and explained quickly that all the military ladies had been evacuated by the British Army the day before. Someone, he didn't know who, knowing I was already in Batavia, had volunteered to pack my stuff and take it along. They had all left on a ship presumably going north from Batavia early that very morning.

He was very concerned for me and suggested I should contact anyone in the Services I knew, without delay. I asked him what he himself, his family, and all the other Dutch people around proposed to do. He said without any hesitation, 'This is our home – we shall make a firm stand. They will never drive us away from here – '

There was a young RAF officer in the bar I knew by sight. I think he was an accountant. When I told him what had happened, he said that my being left behind was inexcusable as there had been time to contact me through HQ in Batavia. He went off to telephone and came back merely to confirm that the ship had in fact sailed at 6 a.m.

He thought it best for me to return at once to Batavia as there was always the possibility of another ship. I asked him about a hospital ship but he said there wasn't much hope since the brutal sinking of one, north of Sumatra. Present policy was against moving badly wounded cases. Everything going north was open to attack and the chances of handicapped men surviving was minimal.

Civilian planes had now ceased to operate in the island but some trains were still running. He found a timetable and consulted it. I wished it were in some way possible for me to stay with Morgan. The thought of my being taken prisoner was the worst worry I could burden him with. He had always had ascendancy over me, I had always been intimidated by his criticism, but here at any rate was a chance for me to show him the stuff of which I was made. It was my turn to show strength and powers of endurance. I was glad.

I telephoned the hospital and asked the sister if I might see my husband as I was obliged to leave. She said, not before the next visiting hour which was the next morning, and hung up.

The accountant had meanwhile been on to the railway station and been told there was no train until the following afternoon which was luckier than I could have hoped for.

I had somehow to get through the next sixteen hours or so until I could see Morgan.

Still wearing the white sharkskin dress I had put on to go to Batavia, I had no change of clothes except for a nightgown in my overnight bag.

There was another man, a tubby middle-aged Army officer, at

the bar while I was talking to the accountant, and he put down his pink gin and butted into our conversation. His wife, he said quite unemotionally, had been killed in a raid about a week ago and he still had all her clothes. If they were any use to me he would gladly bring them round and I could help myself to whatever I wanted.

This sounded like a very welcome and practical diversion. I thanked him and he insisted on buying us another drink. The manager said drinks were on the house from now on and that cheered us all up.

I had some food with the young accountant before the dining-room closed and when I went to my room was surprised to find a strange green cabin trunk already there. The Army man had certainly not wasted any time.

I opened the trunk expectantly and simply could not believe my eyes. It had to be a joke. About nine cocktail dresses of the most ornate variety and a pale mauve suit with matching marabou around the lapels were all the trunk contained and to make things worse the woman must have been at least six feet tall and big with it.

I tried on a black thing with sequins in a draught-board pattern all over. The décolletage reached my navel. I looked like a hideous precocious child 'dressing up'. Giggling and falling about I was trying on a pleated satin with huge sailor collar and couldn't resist adding a rope of fake pearls dangling to my knees when there was a knock on the door and the young accountant stood there, his eyes popping. From somewhere down the corridor came strains of dance music – 'A tisket a tasket, I lost my yellow basket' – and, helpless with laughter, I seized the young man and whirled him round in a quick-step.

He was laughing too now and had his arms right round me, an absurd expression on his face, when I noticed another figure in the doorway.

It was the Chief Medical Officer from Batavia.

'I'm sorry to interrupt,' he said pompously, 'but I came to tell Mrs Morgan that a hospital ship is due in tonight and I intend to get her husband onto it.'

The accountant melted into the background. I heard him scuttling off down the corridor. I caught sight of myself in the long mirror – an absurd figure in the grotesque dress with my breasts half exposed. Beginning to explain about the clothes was getting me nowhere, so I gave up, dragged the cover from the bed and wrapped myself in it.

Thanking the group-captain for the marvellous news, I added that I should be going to see my husband the next morning and would tell him.

The man didn't say anything further but his whole attitude conveyed that he thought me a stupid and wanton woman.

TWELVE

I went out into the town and found a man's clothing shop still open. I bought a pair of natural drill slacks and a small size shirt to match which more or less fitted. As an afterthought I also bought a boy's navy blue sweater of some coarse harsh wool and a tough pair of sandals. When paying for the clothes I begged needle and thread, and back at the hotel spent the rest of the evening cutting several inches off the trouser legs and making new hems.

One of the maids agreed to wash and iron my dress overnight. From the dead woman's trunk I took a remarkably plain and good quality leather belt and this, with my blue scarf, made my practical new outfit less like a uniform.

There was still an awful lot of time to get through. Back in the bar, I found quite a number of people had gathered, but there was no sign of Group-Captain Ryan or any of the staff from the RAF unit. There were several civilian Dutch men and women and some Army officers. The one who had offered me the clothes was not among them and I was relieved for I hadn't the faintest idea what to say to him.

The young accountant came in and apologised for leaving me to the 'Brass Hat Medico' earlier, but added he thought it wiser under the circumstances.

Someone had turned on a radiogram and people started dancing. The accountant was far less shy since our escapade of the dreadful clothes and I was pleased when he asked me to dance with him. It was easier than talking and I didn't want to drink.

I kept looking at the clock and trying to work out exactly how many hours until I could see Morgan. I was just thinking it time to go and try to get some sleep, when I felt a tap on my shoulder. It was the flight-sergeant who had told me about the attack on Palembang. He asked me about Morgan and I told him about the hospital ship.

'You will do everything you can to get him out, won't you?' he pleaded. He was whispering in my ear very earnestly, his manner, like that of the group-captain, inferring that I was behaving badly . . .

'He's a great guy – one in a million – the wing-commander,' he said finally.

'I know,' I answered, feeling exasperated, not trusting myself to say more.

Soon after this incident, although I knew it was too early to try to get some sleep, I went off to my room and sat for a long time in the dark in the open window trying to work out exactly what I would say to Morgan.

I was certainly not going to let on that I had been left behind. The thing to do was establish the fact that he was to be taken off in the hospital ship quite firmly in his mind, and to let him think I was being put on another ship.

Staring out into the black night I remember wondering what Emperor Hirohito was doing at that moment in time.

THIRTEEN

During the night there were two more raids. A bomb was dropped in the main street, and the first thing I saw from my window was a great column of yellowish black smoke reaching into the sky for hundreds of feet; a big oil installation had been hit somewhere beyond the hospital.

There was no water in the taps and no servants about the hotel, but my dress – miraculously laundered – was carefully folded and laid outside my door.

I dressed and made myself as well-groomed as is possible with talcum powder, a hair-brush and a little make-up, and went to find some breakfast. The manager himself was in the restaurant in chef's apron offering fruit juice, slices of cold meat and goat's milk. I drank a cup of milk and ate a small piece of ham and went off to find a taxi. The manager came running after me with a basket of eggs and fruit to take to the hospital. I was so touched by the man's kindness I could have kissed him. Instead, I told him I would never forget his gesture, and I never have.

Nearing the hospital another alert sounded and on arrival I found the big outer doors locked and barred.

The taxi-driver rang the bell many times but no-one answered until about forty minutes later when the all-clear shrilled.

At last, a small grille was opened and a man told the driver –who fortunately spoke a bit of English – that I would be allowed to enter the hospital, but that visiting hours were now over and I must get special permission from the Matron in order to see a patient. Those were the rules.

Admitted, I was led to a waiting room where I was made to wait a further hour before a nurse came to take me to Morgan.

He was lying with a heavy mattress on top of him and he was unsuccessfully striving to keep the weight of it off his legs. It was a ridiculous sight. He told me that this was one of the many crazy air-raid precautions peculiar to the establishment.

The very first night before anyone had done anything for him, a nurse had tried to make him get under his bed – had half dragged him until he had threatened to hit her. The mattress on top was her idea of partial protection.

I heaved and hauled the monstrous thing off him and mopped his face and combed what was left of his hair. He had managed to get into a blue pyjama jacket and his eyes were the same clear vivid blue – the whites clearer than I had ever seen them. This, I thought, was surely a good sign, and somebody must have taken the whisky away.

He knew all about the hospital ship and said he was trying to get permission for me to go with him. I had not thought of this. It was, of course, the perfect answer.

We clung to each other for a few moments muttering nonsenses when a harsh female voice announced that it was time for me to go. I took no notice and the order was bellowed again. Time was up.

By tacit agreement we decided to ignore it. Morgan was now holding on to me so tightly I could have cried out with pain but closed my eyes and pressed my cheek to his rough purple one.

'Get back to Batavia – see the medical bods. All right?' he whispered. Giant hands seized my shoulders, wrenched me up and away. The Amazon nurse frog-marched me out of the room in the direction of the main doors.

The taxi-driver was still there. He grinned when he saw me, then told me that the railway line to Batavia had been bombed that morning. I asked him to take me back to the hotel, paid him generously and thanked him. Someone in the bar said that repairs had already been started on the line. I waited a couple of hours and rang the station. The trains were running again and I caught one at about four o'clock in the afternoon.

Back in the Hotel des Indes in Batavia I was given the same room I had occupied twice before and marvelled at the unshaken excellence of the place. In those days, the Hotel des Indes was the Claridges of the Far East. Everything was beyond reproach: the floors and furnishing spotless; the gardens and little courtyards and window boxes cherished; the dozens of barefoot boys in their snow-white drill with bright cummerbunds moving to carry out every wish and whim; the food exotic and superb. It was without parallel. It made me feel guilty.

Having parked my small bag I went to RAF HQ, and managed, after a certain amount of devious talking, to get myself into the presence of the Chief Medical Officer himself. Much much more authoritative than my GC.

To my surprise he was gentle and charming, said that Morgan was definitely to be sent off on the hospital ship – rather against the advice of the Dutch surgeon who wanted to operate without delay. Then he leaned towards me and to my utter amazement said that he saw no reason why I should not accompany my husband.

On an impressive piece of official paper, he began to write something. Once or twice he glanced up at me questioningly and I wondered if he was remembering the unfortunate incident in the hotel at Bandoeng, but he finished the chit, signed it with a flourish and handed it over to me. It said roughly – 'This officer, Wing-Cdr R. H. Morgan of — Squadron, would benefit from his wife's care and attention during passage to safer territory. Mrs Morgan has had a good basic St John's Ambulance training and considerable nursing experience.'

'Correct?' he asked loudly as he watched me reading it through.

'Yes,' I said boldly, knowing it to be untrue. I had once put a splint on our hamster's leg and it died three days later. That was virtually the only nursing I had ever done.

I put the paper in my handbag. He told me to stay near a telephone at the hotel and wished me luck. The interview was over. I wanted to say something about the silly moment of the trunk of clothes in the hotel at Bandoeng, but decided against it, thanked him for his kindness and left.

There was barely time to get my poor not so white dress

washed and ironed once more and buy a large white handkerchief to tie back my hair, when the call came. An officer, the
young flight-lieutenant from HQ, collected me in a jeep and
drove me down to the docks at Tanjong Priok.

Tanjong Priok was the port area for Batavia, the capital. The
big port of Surabaja on the east coast of Java was already
rumoured to be in Jap hands. That left only the tiny port of
Tjilatjap in the south.

The hospital ship was very small but freshly painted white
with big red crosses on funnel and deck so that there was no
mistaking her. Alongside was a powerful looking American
cruiser.

FOURTEEN

Taken aboard, I was introduced to the doctors and nurses. The latter, even though English, filled me with awe and terrified me every bit as much as the ones in the Dutch hospitals, but soon turned out to be much more sympathetic.

One of them, much younger than the others, was very pretty. She took me to her cabin and told me about the man she was engaged to back home and I told her all about Morgan. She made me feel a lot better by saying that as they were so short-handed I could be a tremendous help on board. There were only five nurses and three doctors to cope with over a hundred bad casualties, she said, and added that I might come in for some criticism and rough treatment. She hoped I wasn't squeamish as I would certainly get all the filthy jobs – bed-pans and such. I had no idea how I would react but I knew I would have a good bash at it or die in the attempt.

We were only waiting for the last few patients from Bandoeng, she explained, and were due to sail at dusk.

I stayed out of the way in the nice nurse's cabin and made swabs for the steriliser and she gave me some snapshots of her fiancé to look at. While I was working, she was sewing a tobacco pouch for one of the doctors which she had cut out of a scrap of rubber sheeting.

At about four o'clock we heard the ambulances arriving on the quay and going to the porthole I saw them drawing alongside. The young doctor for whom the tobacco pouch was being made, poked his head in the door and advised me to lie low until we sailed, promising to let me know when Morgan was safely aboard.

Thunder sounded in the distance and then nearer, so that we knew it was not thunder, but bombs. Bombs followed by gun-fire.

The ship's siren sounded a shrill blast. There was much noise of shouted orders and men running. I thought of the injured men lying on stretchers on the dock or being carried aboard. I wanted to rush out and help – I was really very strong physically – but had hardly put my head out of the cabin when I was ordered to keep out of the way.

This last order came from a much older nurse in tweed skirt and tin hat. She had a string round her neck and attached to it a lump of rubber. This, she suddenly put in her mouth and bit on, then seized me by the arm, pulled me along the deck and down a steep companionway.

At the bottom and to the left, she pushed open a door showing more steps leading down into darkness.

I could hear aircraft right overhead now and as the first of a stick of bombs fell, she pushed me hard so that I flew sprawling into the blackness. Like a cat flung out at night, I went on falling and landed on a slithery mass of some dry shifting granular substance. A moment later the big woman landed heavily close beside me, out of breath and grunting. She must have taken the rubber from between her teeth for I heard her say 'Great place – this. Where we keep the crew rice.'

Silence, except for the woman's heavy breathing and the blood pounding in my ears – then more aircraft, very high and a deafening series of explosions. The ship seemed lifted in a great hand and shaken. The nurse and I were thrown together time and time again and I bit my tongue and felt the salty blood running from the corner of my mouth and saw the purpose of the rubber plug. In between each of the ear-assaulting bursts were sounds of creaking wood, as if the fabric of the vessel could not take the strain and there were sounds too of broken glass and muffled cries.

Again silence for a longish spell, and then the 'all-clear'.

The big nurse heaved herself to her feet, struggled to the step and opened the door. I followed her fearfully on deck. It was incredible to learn that we had not in fact been hit – that the biggest shocks and vibrations had been caused by the cruiser opening fire on the aircraft. They had shot down two into the sea. Most of the medical equipment and a lot of supplies had been smashed, two men on the quay had been injured, but none of the wounded on stretchers had been touched.

Morgan was safely on board, the young doctor came to tell me and to take me to see for myself. I spat on my handkerchief and tried to scrub off the ridiculous blood from the front of my dress but only made it worse.

Not that it mattered. There was very little time or need for explanations of any kind. Morgan wasn't looking too bad. He said I was a clever girl and had I any cigarettes – that life was really very simple and that from now on we had nothing to worry about.

I was kneeling on the floor by his bunk and thinking I'll never be afraid of anything again, that nothing mattered now we were together, when someone tapped me on the shoulder and asked me to go at once to the captain's cabin. I should have ready my papers and nurse's qualifications, the man in Army uniform told me.

I said I had none, other than the recommendation from the Senior MO.

The captain, a wizened little man, cast a desultory glance at this and let it flutter to the floor. Nobody bothered to pick it up. The nice young doctor appeared and said the senior MO on board fully approved of Mrs Morgan being taken on as an orderly as they were so short-handed. The Army man who still had a hand on my shoulder – a major with piggy eyes and a bad-tempered face – pointed out to the captain that unless I had papers proving that I was a registered nurse, I had no right to sail on a hospital ship.

If the enemy stopped and searched the ship they were entitled to sink her if they found a civilian aboard. The captain, who still had not been able to look me in the eye, nodded his agreement and went into an inner cabin.

There was no more to be said.

I asked permission to say goodbye to my husband and the grisly transport officer guided me back to Morgan.

Morgan simply refused to believe what I had to tell him and tried to get out of his bunk demanding to see the captain.

'Get that passenger ashore!' someone yelled. Two people came and restrained Morgan and I was turned and pushed along the deck towards the gangway. Someone handed me my bag. I was pulled and hauled like a sack of potatoes off the ship and into a car. At the hotel I was dumped, with my little canvas grip and my shoes full of rice and the memory of the tell-tale blood oozing from beneath Morgan's dirty bandages as he tried to get to me.

So this is what it means to be truly abandoned, I thought. Nothing could save me from the Japanese now.

FIFTEEN

Later that day, I learned from one of the hotel staff that the captain of the ship had in fact had his Chinese mistress on board all the time. I heard too with mixed feelings, that Morgan had succeeded in getting out of his bunk before they sailed, and had had to be given an injection to put him out.

The little ship left Batavia under a full moon on the evening of 23 February.

Of what happened during the next few days I can't recall anything very clearly. A sort of numbness seemed to overtake me as if induced by some drug, although I took nothing, not even aspirin. I didn't sleep, just lay down at the accustomed time, and got up when it was light. A false lull that sometimes follows shock enveloped me. It was like being another person. I thought of nothing.

Fate had now dealt me a stinging blow. I could only try to accept whatever happened now – try to be calm and philosophical – pray that Morgan would have a safe journey, and that his wounds would heal.

'Something always comes – out of the blue,' said one of the faded Dutch beauties who lived permanently in the hotel. We exchanged pleasantries and inanities in French or English. The news grew worse by the hour.

Every morning I walked down to HQ, hung about, showed my face and waited for instructions. There never were any.

I disliked the man at the front desk. A tall affected homosexual with long side-burns. He should have been in ENSA, I thought. It was obvious he disliked me as much as I did him. One morning in answer to my usual question, he observed in a bleak voice without a shade of emotion, that all the ships leaving Tanjong Priok during the past week had been attacked by the Japanese and most of them sunk.

'That simply cannot be true,' I said. 'What about Geneva Conventions?'

He shrugged, avoided my eyes, and picking up another piece of paper, read me a report about Jap atrocities: 'A shipful of wounded men accompanied by Australian nurses had been sunk off Banka Island on the Sumatra coast. The men who managed to get ashore were all bayonetted on the beach. The nurses wading into the surf from a lifeboat had been machine-gunned.'

'Are you feeling all right? Would you like a glass of water?' another man in the office asked.

Ignoring them both, I walked out. It would take more than this to get me down. Morgan was indestructible. If he was dead I would believe it only when the Air Ministry in London substantiated the fact. Even they had been known to make mistakes.

Plucking a sprig of plumbago from the bush beside the door, I tucked it into my belt and walked slowly back to the hotel.

Perhaps the poor misguided man at HQ was trying to prove that I stood a better chance of survival by not going on the ship.

Perhaps he was a sadist as well.

I did not dwell on the horrors of being taken prisoner by the Japanese. In the back of my mind, I felt that like everything painted black, the actual is rarely as bad as the imaginary.

I felt no inclination to strive any further to get away – just wondered endlessly about Morgan and if I would ever see him again – going over and over in my mind how much better I could have been for him – all the things I had wanted to say and not succeeded in saying to him. I started taking his letters to bed with me. It was all I had of him. I had bought a tough celluloid envelope to keep them in and many times I relived the terrible moment when I had hesitated about packing the bulky package on that first journey to find him in Batavia.

SIXTEEN

When the two men in khaki came and sat down at my table one evening, I could not have cared less. Vaguely registering the fact that they were Australians, I was not surprised when they introduced themselves and began telling me of their escape. They were members of the Australian Command.

They had been on General Gordon Bannet's staff – the CO of the Australian Army in Malaya – and had got away through the enemy lines at night and then in a very small boat until picked up by a British destroyer off the Sumatra coast.

The older of the two, a major, was old enough to have been my father, and had a deeply-lined face and gentle eyes. The younger one, a captain, was brash, talked too much and all the time his eyes roved the room in case anyone more interesting should come in.

They ordered drinks and the older man asked me about myself and started to tell me about his sheep-farm in Queensland. It wasn't of much interest to me but I appreciated his effort to please and entertain me and willed myself to respond.

After a while, the captain, bored with scanning the room, tried to horn in on our conversation and gain attention for himself. Having no success, he suddenly leaped to his feet, seized my hand and said I must show him the town or at least what was left of the night-life.

He made it patently clear that he meant just the two of us but I agreed to go only if the major came too.

We went off in a taxi to the Harmony Club and later to various other less reputable spots, all still astonishingly swinging and noisy. I danced with each of the men in turn. The younger one was an expert and it was fun responding to his lithe movements, not unpleasant to feel a man's arms around me guiding and protecting. If only it could have continued that way. It soon became obvious he was drinking too much. His eyes became bloodshot, his mouth sagged. As soon as I protested that I wanted a rest or to go back to his friend, he would shout 'On-on, drink up!' and drag us on to the next joint.

The last place was so dimly lit it was like going into a cinema. The vague shapes of people, felt, rather than seen, frightened me. They all seemed wild and hell-bent on shedding their inhibitions.

The young Australian put his hand on the back of my thigh, slid the palm firmly upwards and pressed me against him. His breath stank, we struggled and nearly fell over. Someone pushed between us, put an arm round me and led me away. It was the nice major. The captain lurched after us. 'Goodie-goodie,' he mouthed in my ear. I hung on to the older man and took no notice.

Outside, the fresh night air hit us like a bucket of cold water. It was so clean and pure. I said 'Let's walk back to the hotel,' and manoeuvred myself between the two of them linking an arm with each.

We swayed along in step and the air was full of the scent of frangipani and chempaka. I felt curiously serene and as if I were swimming.

Out of the darkness, a taxi appeared heading straight towards us very fast. We all shrank instinctively to the side of the road but the car didn't alter its course and was almost on top of us. I felt myself seized by the major, lifted and thrown. Landing awkwardly, I found myself in a smelly but dry ditch. I scrambled to my feet and peered about. The major was lying on his side out in the road and the captain was kneeling beside him. I felt sick with fright and my legs shook as I limped over to them. At first I was sure the older man was dead. We could still hear the crazy taxi screaming off in the distance. The older man struggled to a sitting position, then managed to get to his feet. He was joking feebly and saying did I think we might get a taxi – any other taxi.

I saw one coming slowly down the road and ran towards it

motioning it towards the others. We helped the major in and told the driver to take us to the Military Hospital.

We had to leave him there for examination. A nurse said she would telephone us at the hotel in the morning. The injury was most likely to be a broken or damaged rib.

The captain and I went back to the hotel in silence. He promised to let me know as soon as he had some news of his friend.

It turned out to be more serious than the nurse had predicted. Several ribs were broken and there was some damage to the lungs. They had no room to keep him in hospital so we both went to bring him back to the hotel.

I felt very badly about him. There is inevitably something very close, very personal about someone who has saved your life.

He refused to stay in bed for long, and I met him later that day in the bar. Looking ashen-faced, he was treating the whole incident as a joke and ridiculed my seriousness and concern. I promised to have dinner with him the following evening, but I never did as he was sent to the south of the island the next morning and I never saw him again.

Months later I made enquiries about him and heard that he was very seriously ill in a hospital in Brisbane. Much later, I heard that he had died.

I felt an agony of guilt over the whole wretched affair. What can one say about a man who has fought the Japanese in the jungle, escaped, suffering terrible hardships only to be run down by a drunken taxi-driver when coming out of a night-club? That he gave his own life for that of an unknown girl he happened to have picked up, is something I could never be reconciled with.

After the major left I began to loathe the idle, demoralising atmosphere of the hotel, to experience a self-disgust and determined to try to get work of some kind.

The Matron of the Military Hospital was neither gracious nor grateful when I went to offer my services, but she did direct me to another hospital in a very poor quarter of the town, for women and children. The cases were mainly skin diseases, eye-infections and some malaria, not that I came much into contact with the patients.

I was received with a certain amount of enthusiasm and

gratitude, but it was obvious that with language difficulties I could only be of use doing menial tasks. I didn't mind. In fact, in the state of mind in which I found myself, the unpleasant and punishing work was exactly what I needed. I scrubbed floors, table tops and bed-pans, unblocked sinks, and from time to time helped clean up babies and older children.

Each evening I walked back to the hotel, scrubbed and disinfected myself, had some food and went to bed exhausted. I was sleeping again without any trouble and felt a great deal better morally and physically, in spite of cracked sore hands and split nails.

Just past midnight one night, after a particularly battering day, I was wakened by the telephone. It must be HQ, I thought at first. It was a man's voice, somehow strangely familiar and in distress. I struggled but couldn't place it. The deep voice said, 'Thank God, at last. It is you. Are you all right?'

My ears and brain exerted themselves and I heard myself saying 'Rob? It's Rob Beresford, isn't it?'

'Yes. I'm here, in the hotel. Can I come and see you?'

'Of course. Right away.'

Scrambling into a wrapper, I brushed my hair and as the cheap cotton garment was very brief, unlocked the door and got back into bed.

Rob Beresford had been at Flying Training School with Morgan in the very early days. They had been posted to different branches of the Service and had lost touch until Rob was posted out to Kuala Lumpur on special duties about a year before the Jap invasion. He used to come down and spend his leave and all his odd week-ends with us in Singapore and I quickly began to see for myself all the qualities Morgan had enthused about in him. He had married very young in England and his wife had died giving birth to their first child. The baby was still-born.

He was of medium height but well-muscled and looked rather like David Niven with his permanently surprised expression, shyness and powers of understatement. When he burst into my room at the hotel that night I was horrified to see how ill and old he looked. He was very emaciated and the hair round his ears was almost white although he couldn't have been much over twenty-four.

He came over and sat diffidently on the edge of my bed and took my hands in his and told me how he had got out of Singapore by the skin of his teeth in a sailing dinghy. He got very wet, he said, but almost died of thirst because the jerry-can of water he had managed to bring with him went overboard. His face had a hunted anguished look and his voice was unsteady. I put my arms round him and hugged him. It seemed the most natural thing in the world to do.

After I had told him about Morgan and the ship and my being left behind, I got out of bed and found the small bottle of whisky I had weakly bought for Morgan and had the strength of mind not to give to him, and we sat there on the bed, very close, sipping the stuff out of tooth mugs, giggling and stroking each other's faces and holding hands.

Rob looked so utterly weary, I made him lie down on my bed and eased off his shoes. Pulling the sheet up to his chin, I kneeled beside him, smoothing his creased forehead, and after a while lay down on the bed close to him for it seemed the most natural thing to do. We lay with our arms around each other and cried like a couple of kids. I don't know what his tears were for – mine were for Morgan, for Rob himself, for the little Chinese girl with the severed head and for the whole futile wretchedness of the war.

I had forgotten how comforting a good howl and being held in someone's arms could be. I sniffed, dried my eyes, blew my nose and told him about working in the hospital. He looked at my ugly hands and kissed the coarse fingers and said better not let Morgan see them that way. He had another drink from the tooth mug, said drinking the old sod's whisky was doing him a power of good, and told me a story about their drinking nights at Mildenhall.

He had lodgings in the town and Morgan used to turn up from time to time to spend the nights with him. The old landlady never minded Morgan's singing and waking up the whole household but used to raise hell because he always drank the morning milk from the doorstep on his way out. We giggled over this and I saw Rob's eyelids begin to droop and presently he slept. After a while I did too until dawn glimmered through the half-closed shutters and cold light penetrated the room.

I got up very quietly and went to the bathroom. When I came back, Rob was dressed and standing by the window smoking a cigarette. I went over to him and kissed him lightly on the cheek and then pressed my face into his shoulder for an instant.

'Someone is bound to see you leaving my room,' I said, 'but don't let it bother you. I'll have to dash now.'

'I'm sorry – but you know, you just about saved me from going round the bend. You're a great girl.'

He put his arms around me once more and held me close, telling me to shut my eyes. When I opened them, he had gone. I listened to his steps receding for a few seconds, heard other footsteps, jocular words. Just as I thought. The titbit of scandal would be all round the hotel in next to no time.

In the infants' clinic that morning I was very tired and thought about the previous night quite a lot. What if I had slept with my husband's best friend? Affection and compassion was all I felt for him, and even if Rob found me sexually attractive he would never abuse such a relationship. Even supposing he had pleaded with me to let him make love to me, I was much too scared of getting pregnant.

Supposing I was caught by the Japanese soldiers and raped? If I absolutely had to have a baby, I thought, as I lifted a year-old Javanese toddler onto the table for an injection, I'd really much rather have one something like one of these with oblique eyes and hair like a lick of black paint.

There was a message for me at the desk when I got back to the hotel. It was from Rob saying he would see me in the bar at seven and that he might have some news for me from HQ.

SEVENTEEN

I saw Rob in the bar that evening. He was with some other Air Force people and was his old casual understating self. He told me rumour had it that we were all going to be sent off down to the south coast. There was some talk of a ship from Tjilatjap.

This news was confirmed later by a call from HQ. I was to report to the railway station at six the following morning. Quite late in the evening I went back to the hospital to explain why I would not be coming to help any more. Two of the Javanese nurses cried and one begged me to write down my name and address in England so that they could send me a birthday card. One of them had found out the date from my passport, it seemed. I was very touched and left the place misty-eyed and saddened.

Avoiding the crowd in the bar when I got back to the hotel, I went straight to my room and sorted out my things for the next day. I had so few possessions it didn't take long, then I went through the bundle of Morgan's letters and burned all but seven of them. The small bonfire on the verandah tiles made an appalling stink and I was conscious of it all night long.

At the railway station, there was a sizeable group of Service personnel and one woman. The woman was Nana. We were both delighted and rushed to embrace each other which called forth a good deal of comment. She started right away on a graphic account of her adventures. She too had eventually left the Tjitrap camp on her own initiative and had managed to get in touch with some friends in Batavia with whom she had been staying.

She had had no news of her husband and had become resigned to his having been taken prisoner in Singapore.

The officer in charge of the party started telling us about the journey. We were to go by train to a place called Poerworkata. There we would spend the night. The next day another train would take us down to the port. It was now the only one not in Japanese hands and it was likely to be attacked at any moment.

The train was old and moved very slowly. We sat upright on sticky, varnished wooden seats like sections in a toast-rack. Rob was more like his old self, flippant and good-tempered, unlike most of the others who were worried or apathetic. As the day wore on even Rob showed signs of strain. Once or twice I caught him looking at me. I had purposely not sat beside him in case we should appear to be too intimate, but now I wished I had. I was glad Nana was with me. She had very sensibly brought a basket of food which she shared very liberally. All I had was a small tin of biscuits bought at the last minute from the hotel bar.

The temperature rose noticeably with every mile and the humidity was intense.

We kept stopping for no apparent reason and twice found ourselves being shunted backwards along the line. Rob said the lines must be damaged and we had to go back to junctions and try other routes. Once we stopped near a small village and were able to buy papayas and bananas.

Three times we heard and saw aircraft overhead, but they were very high and paid no attention to our small train.

After seven hours slow jolting we came to Poerworkata. The men were told to get into a waiting truck. Nana and I were to be taken to a convent near Purbolinggo, the others to a Dutch army camp. At the last minute I found myself minding very much being separated from Rob. We exchanged a last meaningful look.

'Keep safe. God bless,' he said, before we were driven away in a jeep.

Nana needed some help. She was now as round as a cottage loaf and suffered cramp in her legs if she sat still for long. I wished she would wear some more enveloping garment. Her condition was glaringly obvious and aroused considerable interest and speculation which she seemed to enjoy but I did not.

EIGHTEEN

The convent was also a school for Javanese girls of good family and was run by Dutch nuns. In their undemonstrative way they made us very welcome. They gave us a room each and showed us where we could wash from tubs of rain water. When we had washed and tidied ourselves up, one of the novices came to tell us that supper was ready.

It was a simple meal of rice and fish and the older girls waited on us, smiling and laughing over our language difficulties. None of them spoke anything but Dutch and Javanese. One of the sisters, we were made to understand, spoke French but she was away at a mission hospital.

The Mother Superior said a special prayer over us before we went to bed. We heard the word 'Tjilatjap', but that was all we could understand.

I didn't sleep much. The mosquitoes were vicious, the bed hard and prickly. I was glad when we were called to have some tea and rough flat bread like a rubbery pancake. The jeep was already waiting for us beyond the oleander hedge, one of the girls told Nana. We thanked the nuns, said goodbye to them all, and were driven off in a great cloud of dust.

At the station, a Dutch Army officer came running towards us along the platform saying there had been a mistake about the time. The train had already gone. Our driver must now try driving us across country to another line where we might still get a train to the south.

I hung on to Nana, keeping her as steady as I could, as in a suffocating heat we bounced and bumped along the winding dusty road. I was terrified she would have a miscarriage. After about two hours we came down a road running parallel to another railway line and saw a station ahead. The driver pointed to a bench, hauled out our bags, turned the jeep around and left us.

It was now about noon. The temperature must have been well over a hundred and the mosquitoes swarmed about us. I begged one of Nana's nauseating Egyptian cigarettes to ward off the lethal insects but they minded the smell less than I did.

Nana was looking surprisingly well and unruffled. She laughed at my discomfort, lit another of the odious cigarettes, and said I had a very sexy mouth. I took out my compact and looked at myself. My lower lip, badly stung, was twice its normal size, the skin near to splitting. I could see what she meant. This was no time to be looking voluptuous.

After about an hour we heard the sound of a train in the distance. It was a more civilised passenger train than the one we had travelled in the day before. It was empty except for mounds of luggage. A guard beamed at us when we said 'Tjilatjap' so we got in, spread our belongings and the train chugged off. After a few minutes it stopped and the guard came back to see us. He and Nana had a chat in some language unknown to me and he beamed again and patted her arm.

I had noticed before, this way she had with men, humouring and flattering them to her own advantage. I could learn a lot from her.

I asked her what the guard had to say and she told me he had warned her that he wasn't sure how far the train would take us but that he would do his best to help us on our way.

She had never told me much about herself except about her work in the cabaret and life with her husband in India before they came to Malaya. She looked more Jamaican than anything and yet I learned that she was in fact Anglo-Indian. Her mother had been a *nautch* girl in Bombay, her father, whom she had never seen, a sailor from West Hartlepool.

'I am not educated like you,' she said to me quite early on, 'but I am full of feminine instinct and not afraid of any man.'

She also said, apropos of nothing in particular, 'All good-looking men are bad in bed. The ugly ones are much better. Much better husbands and lovers too.'

When she wasn't eating, or smoking the sickly cigarettes, she smelled her 'smelling-salts', contained in an old-fashioned green glass bottle full of violet-coloured miniature camphor balls. I hadn't seen such an object since I was a very small girl in my grandmother's house.

The landscape we were passing through was mostly flat scrub with stunted palms, with only the occasional patch of verdant green cultivation. I kept myself cheerful by reminding myself that every mile brought us nearer and nearer the coast.

After chugging along very slowly for about another hour we were suddenly jolted out of our seats and heard a great squealing and grinding of brakes.

Putting my head out of the window, I was astonished to see a British Army officer standing at the side of the track pointing ahead. I looked but could see nothing. I called out to him and in a very Sandhurst voice he said 'Surprise-surprise! Hello there.'

The line had apparently been destroyed. Although we were not at all what he had expected, he had a car on the road and would take us down to the port.

Nana asked him about the luggage on the train. He muttered something rude about scattering it among the poor of the district and helped us down with our own cases which he carried, striding ahead of us over the scratchy foliage. Nana waved and blew kisses to the train driver and guard, and followed me across the ditch.

About a hundred yards on, we came to a road. There we found a jeep with American markings, and two more British officers asleep in the back seat. We told the first officer how we came to be on the train and he said he had had a signal to look out for RAF personnel on their way to join a ship at the port. He believed it was still there waiting.

Nana brightened at once and started telling him about her husband. We all squeezed into the front seat and set off.

It turned out to be only about ten miles to the sea, but when we drove through the town to the docks we were told the ship had sailed five hours before. Our friends in the jeep could do no more to help us. They had to report elsewhere in the town. The men in the back had woken up now. One of them suggested we should find the consul's house.

Nana was all for hanging around the docks in case another ship of any kind should come in. I couldn't stand the steaming heat of the place. It was more sinister than Palembang. A ghost port. To the left were the main quays and to the right an oil jetty – all deserted. The rows of great godowns were locked and silent-looking as if they hadn't been used for some considerable time. There was something evil about the long trailing stemmed convolvulus growing about the doors, tall spinifex grasses sprouting between bollards.

I liked even less the few wild lecherous-looking seamen loitering about the waterfront.

We asked an elderly Dutchman in an office on the jetty whether a number of English Air Force men and soldiers had come into the port and left on the last ship. He said only some wounded Dutch had gone aboard. I realised then that Rob and the others must still be at Poerworkata. If all else failed I must try to rejoin them.

Nana asked him if there was somewhere we could get a drink and something to eat and he directed us to a crowded and noisy coffee-shop further along the quays.

At one table under a huge *punka* fan, was a group of Europeans I couldn't place at all. A tall flabby man, corpulent, with a very pale face seemed to dominate two men in brightly patterned shirts and a big woman with auburn hair and a lot of phoney jewellery. Nana told me that they were members of a famous circus she had once worked with in Calcutta, left me, and hurried over to be greeted with endearments and shrieks of delight. They were all rather drunk and talking at the tops of their voices.

I decided to slip away and go and look for the consul's house.

The scene reminded me all too vividly of the drunken night in Batavia and I was in no mood for it.

I had heard that this town was built on reclaimed swamp and that it was only a few miles from the equator. The climate was reputedly one of the unhealthiest in the world and quite unsuitable for Westerners. I had certainly never come across such humidity. It was like being in a foetid Turkish bath. My body ran with sweat. I reckoned the temperature must be about a hundred and thirty and the humidity about the same.

Away from the seamy port area the town itself had a sort of sultry elegance with broad tree-lined avenues and some good looking houses. I began to feel better.

NINETEEN

After a lot of walking up and down and showing my passport to various serious-looking Dutchmen, I found the consulate.

It turned out to be an ordinary modest stone-faced villa with a pretty loggia in front and bougainvillea growing everywhere in profusion. The doors stood open and it looked abandoned.

In the entrance hall was a black console table with a dwarf palm in a brass pot. On the wall an awful painting of a sunset over a tropical bay.

From the back of the house came sounds of hilarity. The Javanese servants were having a party. I wandered through the hall and into a room which might have been an unsuccessful dentist's waiting room. Dilapidated horsehair chairs and a long sofa covered in faded, regency-striped satin. Through a window looking onto a courtyard I could see boys in shorts and some in sarongs lying about eating or drinking. A child was helping herself to cheese straws from a tin with a Fortnum and Mason label. On the way out I saw a *Blackwood's Magazine* lying on a coffee table.

If the servants had seen me, they had no intention of doing anything about it. I left them to their celebration and went back to find the old man on the jetty.

I asked him if he knew where there was an Army camp or depot and after various misunderstandings he drew a little map on the back of an envelope, then darted out and stopped a ramshackle lorry which he said would give me a lift to the place.

It turned out to be an American stores depot just outside the town. The personnel was preparing to pack and move out, up into the hills, they said. I spoke to one of the older men and asked if he could help me get back to Purbolinggo. He suggested it would be wiser to stay and take a chance along with them. There was now no question of escape for anyone, he reckoned. When I persisted, he said there was plenty of spare transport. I could help myself to any of the civilian cars outside the depot fence.

There was a big Ford, not unlike the one I had had in Singapore, only a four-seater. I checked the petrol gauge which showed almost full, then turned it about a few times practising the gear change, then set off back towards the town to find the road on which we had come in that morning. I debated whether to go back and look for Nana to see if she wanted to go with me, but decided in her condition she was probably better off with her own kind of show-business people.

The road was easy enough to find but much narrower and more twisting than I remembered. During the first few miles I had any number of encounters with wide spindly bullock-carts. Each time I met one I put my head out of the window and yelled 'Purbolinggo?' Sometimes I got a grin and hearty 'Ya-ya', but mostly, the driver would look scared to death and ignore me.

It began to grow dark much earlier than I expected and I found that my watch had stopped. I knew that even when I found the small town it would not be easy to find the convent. Perhaps I would do better to make for Poerworkata and look for the army camp. Better still, the railway station at which we had arrived from Batavia. Round the next bend the road looked vaguely familiar, I told myself, and over the next hump-backed bridge, sure enough, a sharp right-angled turn showed the rough surface running parallel to a shallow embankment with single track lines.

By this time I was feeling not only utterly weary but my head ached, the mosquito bites swelled and itched horribly, and I could feel the blood beating at my temples in a most peculiar way I had never experienced before. I hoped I hadn't contracted malaria but doubted if symptoms could develop so rapidly.

As always in those parts, night fell like a curtain and it was with tremendous relief I saw the first houses of the village before total blackness shrouded everything.

I found the railway station without much trouble but as before, it was deserted.

My only hope now was to find my way back to the convent. I could hear explosions a long way away but had no idea whether they were bombs or gunfire or from which direction the sounds were coming.

I was beginning to be very frightened and shaky. While turning the car, the lights failed and the engine stalled. I tried the ignition again and again but it was no good. Switching off, I waited, in case I had flooded the carburettor, but to no avail. I had no idea how far I had driven. It was possible I was out of petrol.

There was now only one thing to do. Leave the car and find the convent on foot.

Carefully, I have no idea why, I wound up all the windows and locked the thing before picking up my bag and setting off. I had already worked out that at the end of the straight flat road north of the station, I had to turn left, cross a bridge and several miles further on take a turn to the right. I was quite clear about the road, but I must give my eyes time to become accustomed to the dark. I stood quite still with my back to the car blinking and waiting.

TWENTY

To my surprise I found after a short time that I could see quite well. At first I'd cautiously slid my feet along the ground at each step, but now it was no longer necessary. I could make out the road ahead quite plainly and the darker strips at either side which were the ditches.

My bag grew heavy and my heels grew sore after about a couple of miles, but all told I felt better being out in the open air, and confident that I would soon be safely in the convent. Once I leaped in the air at a furtive rustling from the ditch, but it turned out to be a straying goat which bleated tremulously in answer to my voice.

I don't know how many times I fell into holes, how many times I picked myself up from my hands and knees, but the distance was unimportant when I rounded a bend and saw ahead the high oleander hedges of the convent. I stopped then and listened. I could hear voices – orders being called in harsh male tones in what I thought sounded like Dutch – and the sound of nailed boots marching on the road.

Down in the port I had heard stories from the British soldiers that there were quite a lot of Dutch Fifth Columnists working with the Japs. Surely neither the Japanese nor the Fifth Columnists would invade the convent? Perhaps they were guarding it? Unlikely. The realisation of what stupidity I had been guilty of struck me like a blow on the head. I couldn't turn back. There were soldiers now behind me. I began to shake with fright. I prayed rather weakly that the poor nuns had been evacuated. The convent was now most definitely a Fifth Columnist camp.

Staggering blindly forward, the next thing I knew was that I was leaning on a bayonet.

Sweating and trembling I tried desperately to find any Malay words which might be understood in all the noise and confusion. I dropped my bag and groped for it but someone seized me from behind and I straightened up. Someone else reached out for me, freed me and guided me forward.

The man behind me started to laugh and I half-turned and could see his teeth and eyes gleaming in the light from a lamp on the building ahead. I recognised the bell-shaped lantern over the convent doorway. One of the soldiers rang the bell and we waited.

From inside the sound of someone crying was ominous. The first soldier carrying my bag ushered me in. I could see now that he was wearing the green-grey of the Dutch army. I stopped.

Something was very wrong. It all seemed oddly different. No pictures or flowers now. All was stark and bare and there was a powerful smell of disinfectant.

On a bench were three elderly well-dressed Dutch women and an old priest. It was one of the women who was sobbing, on and on like a tired child who has been crying for a long time. The old man sat motionless with a book open in his hands but he was not reading it.

The soldier gave me a shove and pointed to a room at the end of the hall. I walked where he indicated and went into the room. He followed and stood a few paces behind me.

An officer in more or less the same colour uniform but in his case immaculately pressed and with a well-cut mandarin collar, sat behind a desk speaking into a telephone.

He had a full face, the skin ochre-tinged, the eyes like black marbles. A thin cord hung from the top button of his tunic with what looked like a bunch of tooth-picks hanging from it and he had a lot of medal ribbons. On a nail on the wall behind him hung a service hat. It had the soft high crown and flexible eye-shade peak that I had only seen before in photographs. It took me several seconds more for my woolly brain to register that the man who was about to question me was Japanese. The uniform was that of the Kempetei. The Japanese Gestapo.

TWENTY-ONE

He put down the receiver and looked at me, his eyes cold, the lashless eyes clicking like a camera shutter. I had the feeling that I was being assessed, recorded, by a computer. He had his hands flat on the desk, the fingers square at the tips, the nails as neat and clean as a surgeon's.

Quite politely, in staccato but perfect English, he told me that I was now under his protection and that I would be well advised to answer his questions and do as I was told. He asked my full name and wrote it down on a pad. Then he asked what had brought me to this island, my husband's name, rank and serial number and his present whereabouts. I told him everything but the latter.

He thanked me and said I should now be given a room and wait until further instructions were issued.

So, this was it. The canker had reached the heart of Java. I would be sent to a prison camp, perhaps back to Singapore or more probably Japan.

I started to ask questions but he appeared to be no longer aware of my existence, simply staring robot-like into the middle distance and tapping a drum beat with his pencil on the desk edge. I felt pinned to the spot with misery and fright. The Japanese officer shouted an order and a soldier came into the room and pulled me out by an arm, across the hall where the old woman was still wailing. He led me down a corridor, up some dark stairs and into a lofty narrow room with a small high grille.

There was a rush mat on the floor and a small table with a carafe of water and an oil lamp on it. The walls were painted a dank dark green and the atmosphere was clammy. The door slammed behind me and the key turned in the lock. With relief I saw my bag in a corner. No doubt they had been through it.

Although it was obvious it had been searched, the money was still there, in an envelope-shaped purse. Someone had helped themselves to most of the biscuits, but the letters had not been touched.

I lay down on the mat and tried to think to some purpose. It was unbearably hot and airless and I couldn't get into any position in which the blisters on my heels didn't hurt. I could hear Morgan's voice caustic and clear as if he were in the room saying 'Nice work. It takes real brilliance and initiative to walk straight into enemy hands. Original anyway!'

Through a miasma of pain, fatigue and hopelessness, I became aware of a scratching sound at the door. The key was turned and a small pale-robed nun came in. She had brought me a bowl of soup and a piece of bread.

I mimed my need to wash and she smiled, nodded, went out and spoke to a soldier in the passage then led me by the hand round a corner and down another corridor to a hole in the concrete latrine. While I was there, she fetched me a bowl of water and a small towel. It was better than nothing.

She stayed near at hand, smiling while I did my best to clean myself, a gentle little mouse of a woman, then led me back to my cell. The soldier locked the door again.

The soup had a sharp sweet-sour taste, like beetroot with vinegar and sugar, but to my surprise I found I was ravenous and finished it up, wiping the bowl with the tough bread. Then I lay down again and reflected on all the wretched things I had done in my life.

I had been ambitious and wild, inconsiderate and ungrateful towards my parents, often cruel to my mother. Sometimes I had been devious and often petulant with Morgan, and I had rarely done anything in life not motivated by selfishness. How long, I wondered, would it take me to achieve a serenity, absolute patience and selflessness like the little nun?

A lethargy began to steal over me and I must have slept then for several hours.

The next thing I remember was light slanting through the high grille and hearing the sounds of marching feet on the road outside. Javanese troops in retreat or the Japanese taking over? I was agonisingly stiff and hurt all over. My heels were raw and sensitive to every movement, but the mosquito-bite swelling had gone down considerably.

Putting the lamp and water carafe on the floor, I dragged the none too sturdy table under the grille, placed my canvas hold-all on top of it and found as I had hoped, that by standing on top of the lot, could just see out of the high aperture.

The soldiers in the drive below were all wearing the uniform of the Dutch and Javanese. None of them looked the least like the man who had questioned me, but I could be wrong. This could of course well be one of the Fifth Columnist camps.

Faint scratchings at the door came again and I almost fell, but recovering my balance, managed to scramble down and re-arrange the furniture just before the key was turned.

It was a different nun this time with more of the stale pancake bread and some thick gritty coffee. Twice more during the day, I was led to the hole-in-the-floor lavatory, and twice given food. When I showed pleasure at the sight of an orange, the woman came back with a second one, secreted in her robe.

Towards evening, the first nun came back and told me in laborious halting French that I was to be medically examined before being sent to another camp.

An hour or so later, the door was unlocked, flung open with a crash and two soldiers with rifles came to fetch me. The first thing I noticed was that they had both been drinking. Their breath was foul and one of them lurched and staggered.

I was marched this time down the corridor, out of the front door, and round the side of the building to a separate smaller house at the back. The room must at one time have been a music room, for there was still an upright piano piled with books and sheet music, against one wall. Now it was fitted up as a clinic with a long table, a weighing machine, a cabinet of medical supplies, and a doctor's couch with rubber sheeting.

There was no sign of a doctor. I wondered how long I would have to wait.

The little nun told me to take off my clothes and put on a sack-shaped hospital gown. I looked at the soldiers, back at the nun and said I would undress when the doctor arrived and the soldiers had gone.

One of the soldiers – the more drunken of the two, with a fat greasy face and bloodshot eyes bustled the frail little woman out of the room, picked the shift from the floor and threw it towards me, indicating in the clearest possible gestures that I should put it on. I stood quite still, ignoring them. They looked at each other and laughed loudly, then put two chairs against the wall and sat down. One of them produced a bottle from his pocket and drank from it. I closed my eyes and in the next few seconds the possibilities of what might be about to happen to me flashed through my mind. I would be baited, tortured, and finally held down and raped. Where was my Japanese inquisitor of the night before? If I screamed, fought, made enough of a struggle, would someone in authority come?

I opened one eye and saw the bottle being passed from one to the other. If they drank enough they would be shortly incapable of anything. I was wrong.

The bottle clattered to the floor and the smell of saké, the spirit distilled from rice, rose to my nostrils. The man nearest to me lunged to his feet and pulled at my dress. I shrank away from him and saw the other man seize something small and shiny from the table. With one flicking movement he slit my dress from neck to hem and yanked it from my shoulders. They both sat down again and exploded with laughter, brandishing the small silver blade for me to see.

By a movement of his head, the slasher indicated that I should take off my bra and pants. I hesitated a second too long and the knife flicked again, cutting the straps. An involuntary flinch and the descending blade caught the tip of my left nipple. Blood spurted and flowed although I felt no pain. Quickly I pulled down my brief calico knickers and waited. They both leered, swaying slightly.

'Eengleesh Mees velly plittee,' one said and they both clapped their hands and took another drink.

The telephone on the table rang viciously and the little nun came hurrying in. On seeing me she made the sign of the cross and draped my dress over me before answering it. She only spoke three or four words and I couldn't understand one of them.

'*Où est le médecin? Le commandant?*' I asked her, but all she would say was '*Il ne vient pas.*'

'*Alors, c'est fini?*'

'*C'est fini,*' she said and, covering me with her voluminous skirt, spoke pleadingly to the soldiers. One of them was almost asleep, the other still gulping from the bottle. She led me back to the other building and to my room.

The anticlimax was unnerving. I started to giggle with relief as I tore up a handkerchief and stemmed the dripping blood. Morgan always used to say my nipples were like jelly babies.

The nun went away and came back with some iodine and cotton wool and having cleaned the wound and put on a dressing of sorts, I found a clean bra in my bag and began to feel better. I made up my mind to try and get away from the place. I was a fool ever to have left the coast. I would do my utmost to get back.

After the nun had gone, I waited until the sound of her footsteps died away and then cut a small square piece of material from the skirt of the ripped dress. With the needle and thread from the Bandoeng shopkeeper, I sewed a pocket on the inside of my strongest pair of cotton briefs. Into it I pressed as many folded fifty guilder notes as it would hold and, securing the top of the pocket with a safety pin, put them on. Next I dressed in the drill slacks and thin shirt, bound my heels with the remaining strips of handkerchief linen, lay down to get some rest and wait for the other occupants of the establishment to settle for the night.

All my life I had believed that freedom was more important than safety. I knew very little about life in Japanese prison camps except that the Japanese were interested in carrying out experiments on human beings.

I knew that I had to have a stab at getting away even if they caught me again. Even if they shot me, I had to try.

TWENTY-TWO

The sounds gradually lessened. After about two hours, there was only a distant coughing, and a new, louder noise of bull-frogs, their oboe-like music endearingly bold and normal.

Once more, and this time with the utmost care to maintain silence, I manoeuvred the table into position under the high window grille, piled the things on top, climbed up and peered out. There was a half moon with clouds passing rapidly across it but enough light for me to be able to make out that there was only one soldier on guard at the gates. He appeared to be asleep, sitting slumped against the wall, his rifle propped upright against the wall beside him.

If I could clasp the sill and keep my balance long enough I should be able to open the window. With another mammoth effort I could get one knee up and then it would be easy. But how to haul up my grip when I needed that for standing on?

Knotting my belt, the scarf and a piece of ribbon from the bundle of letters together, I passed it through the handles of the bag and with a safety pin attached the ends to the hem of my shirt.

I had to be quick and quiet. The rolled hessian mat gave me another four or five inches. I took three long deep breaths and sprang. In one movement I managed to clasp the middle bar and get a knee grip on the deep sill. My face was squashed against my thigh and for a few seconds I couldn't breathe – then with thumb and first finger of my other hand I contrived to push up the lever which opened the grille. How stupid I thought, to have a window without glass. Contorting my limbs in the most excrutiatingly painful skin-grazing series of wriggles, I found myself half-out, hanging down over the outer sill.

The soldier at the gates had not moved, even the frogs had stopped croaking. I judged the drop to be about twelve feet, the ground sloping away from the wall of the building making the landing even more frightening. I had fallen off many a hay-stack higher than this when I was a child on holiday at the farm, I reminded myself. Making sure that the makeshift cord fastened to my bag was not caught up – by hauling on it and gripping the bag between my feet – I started to wriggle forward until gravity took over and I fell head first into the night. I must somehow have turned over for I landed very heavily on my bottom. A searing pain shot up my spine and came out of the top of my head. The world span round. I felt numb, then sick, then waves of jabbing pins and needles gripped and shook me and I began to roll about in agony and terror. God alone knew what I had broken. I managed not to cry out and surprisingly after a while I lay still and felt better.

Experimentally I tried moving each limb in turn and they all worked. I could hear sounds of someone stirring at the back of the house. I detached my bag, stuffed the line into a corner of it and began to crawl slowly towards the oleander hedges.

Nearing the main gates, I stepped out onto the drive and was perplexed to see that the guard had disappeared. A few seconds later, venturing out onto the road, I saw the back view of him patrolling the hedge along the road to the left, his gun on his shoulder. I seized my bag and sprinted as hard as I could manage in the opposite direction. After about a hundred yards, I dived for the ditch and lay down flat.

Winded and a bit hysterical I soon began to feel an exhilaration at being free and out in the comparatively cool night air. One thing was certain. I really knew this road to the coast like the back of my hand. Where there is a port there is always hope of a boat of some kind. I was a fool ever to have left it. I would do my utmost to get back there.

How far I walked once I got going that night, I have no idea, but by morning when the sun came up, I knew by the sight of the first small village that the distance was negligible. At one of the little *attap* huts I offered money and asked for food. The woman giggled shyly but seized the money and brought me some smelly dried fish and chapati and a bowl of goat's milk. Hurrying away, dragging a child by each hand, she brought back other women and two very old men to see me. They stood in a row and watched me as I ate. When I had finished they smiled and waved me on my way and one small boy ran after me and gave me a slice of papaya which I accepted gratefully, then realised he too, hoped for money. I put a few small coins into his upturned palm and his face split into a grin and he shot off waving his fist in triumph.

One of my heels was very sore and I limped on only a few miles more until I reached a tiny vineyard where I rested for a while in the green shade. Unfortunately, the mosquitoes liked the spot too and I got badly bitten. With lips and eyelids swelling again, I dragged myself off along the dusty road.

It was savannah-type country I was crossing. I was lucky not to be traversing rain-forests in this island.

For several miles after the vineyard, I met no-one. I had to stop from time to time to rebind my heel and one of the toes on the other foot, and once I cupped my hands and drank from a little spring bubbling out of the rocks near a stream.

The stillness of the landscape was uncanny. The monotony of the sandy road mesmerised my senses; the heat of it fried my feet and filled my eyes with grit. Up a slight incline, down another, undulating endlessly. The sun never let up – stayed right overhead in a cloudless sky – a sun that slapped the skin with an almost physical force. Hair and eyes stinging with dust, lower lip swelling so that it pulled away from the gum, I was at last so stricken, I had to sink down and rest.

I resolved to stay there until dark, then press on as far as I possibly could go. After a while, I ate two of the precious biscuits remaining in my tin, took off my shoes, and lay down flat under a eucalyptus tree just off the road. The mosquitoes began attacking me again but as long as I didn't scratch and break the skin, the swellings would, I knew, eventually subside.

A sudden rustling in the grass bothered me more – were there snakes here? A grey-green fish-shape darted from under a stone and I saw with relief it was only a lizard. It looked at me with interest and vanished. I dozed, sweating and aching, but reminding myself that I was alive and free. Anything was still possible.

Morgan, Morgan – if only you could see me now! You always said I had no real guts. I'll show you. I'll make you take that back. You'll see.

TWENTY-THREE

About noon on the seventh day, I reached the outskirts of Tjilatjap. I must have walked about 140 miles. There was a Javanese with a hat like a soup-plate selling fizzy orange coloured drinks from a push-cart. I drank two small glasses of the stuff without taking breath. It was saccharin sweet and reminded me of the bags of sherbet powder we used to buy with a tube of liquorice sticking out of one corner to suck through.

Licking the sediment from the edge of the glass, I looked up to see a lorry with RAF roundels passing at speed. I ran out into the road shouting and waving. There were some airmen in khaki in the back of the vehicle. None of them took the slightest notice. The Javanese came pleading for his glass back and I picked up my grip and trudged on until I came in sight of the quays.

The wizened old Dutchman in his hut on the jetty was still there and seemed pleased to see me. He fanned me with a pearly paper fan and offered me his high wooden stool, helping me on to it, taking my bag, dusting it off with a rag and putting it down with care in a corner. I almost wept at his courtesy. I tried to ask him about Nana and whether he had seen any RAF people but couldn't make him understand.

Just then, I saw a British Army corporal crossing the paved area between us and the water's edge, and called out loudly to him. He looked across at me, his expression a mixture of pleasure and mistrust, asked in a thick Scots accent what the hell I was doing in a place like this and could I do with a cup of tea? One of his mates was just brewing up behind some crates near the godowns. He indicated the spot. Leaving my bag with the

Dutchman, I walked over with him. He told me that there was a ship stuck on a sandbank around the bend of the river before it widened into the estuary. There was hope that the next tide would lift her off. He and two of his mates were in charge of a party of casualties – most of them stretcher cases from a hospital near Sourabaya. There was a chance they could be taken off on this temporarily grounded ship along with some Air Force cases due to arrive from the north.

That could account for the lorry which had passed me on the road. I asked him if he had seen Nana, but he knew nothing of her whereabouts. He remembered seeing her many times in the clubs in Singapore. 'Cor!' he said, 'if my lot knew that little darlin' were around reckon they'd be off of them stretchers like nobody's business!'

The tea which he fetched for me in a monstrous enamel mug was the colour of floor polish, tasted powerful, metallic and very British. I sipped it gratefully, scalding my throat which I hoped the shy soldiers would think the cause of my tears.

Leaving my grip with the old Dutchman, I went off to look for Nana. She was still at the Chai-kana, but alone now except for the proprietor, and looked as if she was nursing a hangover. The circus people had gone with a Dutch orchestra further along the coast to Jogja Karta. Nana, having heard the rumour about the boat on the sandbank, had opted to stay and the café owner had given her a bed. She was touchingly happy to see me and at once assumed that everything was now going to be perfectly simple.

She led me up to her room and began decking herself out for the trip. I sank down on the bed, taking advantage of this however brief period of rest and let her get on with it. I could barely keep my eyes open but fought off sleep and watched indulgently the little barrel-like figure pirouetting around in a pink lace blouse, fish-net stockings, trying on skirt after skirt to find the one she could still fasten over her swelling tummy.

I was a disgrace, she said, letting myself go the way I had. I must clean myself up for the trip – we owed it to those poor wounded fellers to look as nice as we could. I hadn't the heart to say that there was little chance of our being given a place on board even supposing the ship got off the sandbank.

Nana contrived an intricate new upswept hair style and tucked an artificial rose behind one ear. I washed my face and hands and combed my matted dirty hair. I offered to do her packing while she said goodbye to her friend the café owner. She had far too much useless stuff and it was my intention to decide on the more practical of her garments and other possessions, get them into one of her suitcases and stuff the fripperies into another which I could dump without much compunction when the need should arise. If we had the good luck to be taken aboard any ship now, we should certainly not be allowed more than one piece of baggage.

Unfortunately, she caught me half-way through and told me to mind my own business and started all over again, packing everything – the silver shoes, the marabou, black lace nightgowns, boxes and boxes of eyelashes and a ridiculous object which she said was a back-scratcher given her by the Maharajah of Johore.

When Nana asked me what had happened to me during the past few days, I answered evasively, almost tersely. I felt ashamed of my fruitless and stupid efforts and met her questions with questions about herself and her drinking companions instead.

She was no fool and looked at me contemptuously, so that I became self-conscious and looked at myself in the cracked looking-glass over the washbasin.

My face was still swollen around one eye and both lips and it was burned a deep brown except for the tip of my nose and cheek-bones which were bright pink and threatening to peel. My hair was bleached almost silver on top of the head but darker than usual with sweat where it clung to the skin at the temples and round the ears.

To please her, I combed it again and put on some lipstick. Examining my wounded nipple, I found it had not gone septic. It was misshapen but the surface had healed over.

She went on watching me, shrugged and sniffed, and after a final pat to her own coiffure, we went downstairs.

The proprietor insisted we should eat something before we

went down to the docks and generously produced plates of fried rice and a garlic-laden sauce. I didn't feel at all hungry and had become aware of a nagging pain somewhere deep in my lower abdomen, but didn't want to hurt the man's feelings. I managed to swallow a few mouthfuls but refused anything to drink. I hoped to God I hadn't contracted dysentery from some of the fly-blown drinks I had gulped down recently.

I determined to ignore the pain. It would pass off in time like the itch of the mosquito bites. Other things were more important. My feet, for a start. They hurt and throbbed so much I found it hard to keep still. I longed to inspect them, to bathe them, but there was no time and at least they were still covered and were, I hoped, protected from infection.

When Nana had finished her wine, her café-owner friend hailed a rickshaw for us, another for her luggage, and at last we set off for the quays.

TWENTY-FOUR

To our amazement, we saw that a ship had indeed come in. It was a lump-in-the-throat moment for – we admitted to each other later – we hadn't really believed the rumour.

It was a very old and shabby ship, about half the size of a Channel boat, and it was very low in the water. From the number of people scrambling about on its decks it seemed already overcrowded.

Near the gang-plank was a small group of young airmen and a squadron-leader I had not seen before. The airmen could have been some of those without inoculations I had encountered in Bandoeng. Their faces were blank, childish, and in spite of the heat they huddled together sheepishly.

Nana asked the squadron-leader about our chances of being taken on board. The officer said there was room only for badly wounded now, but of course he would see to it that we were taken care of. I asked about the young airmen and from the barely perceptible shaking of his head I gathered they would be left behind. I felt terrible. They looked like animals in a pen waiting to go to the abattoir, clinging together, not understanding.

I asked where the ship was going but he said only the master knew that, but that it would be as far away from this bloody island as possible. As soon as the other wounded cases had been put aboard, we should be sailing. Nana asked if he himself would be going but he said no, he would be returning to his unit in the hills where they would be joining up with some of the Dutch guerrillas.

Retrieving my bag from the watchman's hut and saying a fond goodbye to my old friend, I got back just in time to see four men on stretchers and three on crutches being helped aboard.

At last, when the light was beginning to fail, we were summoned to go up the gangway. I didn't offer to help as Nana hastily did some repacking and abandoned one of her suitcases. There was a good deal of raucous laughter and wolf whistling as she salvaged saucy bits of underwear and scarves and stuffed as much as she could into one case, and when she found she couldn't even lift it, there was a crowd of eager helpers.

On deck, we had to pick our way over rows of prostrate bodies. Very few of them had a pillow, just some rolled up garment on which to rest bandaged heads. Some looked very ill, others astonishingly cheerful. The man who came to take charge of us was an RAF sergeant with a leg in a splint but reasonably mobile. He was a north-countryman, an engineer, and was, he told us, to be a member of the crew. His name was Bert.

Nana's pink blouse and fishnet stockings brought forth more wolf whistles as we wound our way, humping our bags. By this time I was struggling with her enormous tin suitcase and had given her my small grip. We went down to a lower deck then up a steep companionway to our allocated space.

It consisted of a very tiny cabin no more than a cupboard, and a roped-off area of deck about four feet square on the poop-deck.

The cabin was dark and thick with dust and stale crumbs. There was one bunk and two stained mattresses. I heaved one of these out, opting to sleep under the stars.

We sailed at dusk on April 4. There was to be an almost full moon and we would without doubt be spotted by patrolling aircraft. We left by the shallow mangrove-fringed channel which we were told was only normally used in daylight and by small native craft.

Mercifully it began to get cooler, and after the terrible heat of the day this was blissful. We had yet to learn that in the small hours it got so cold that the only coverings we had, two filthy small blankets and Nana's fake fur coat, would be miserably inadequate.

I worked out for myself that if we navigated out of the harbour and then went straight ahead, away from the coast into the Indian Ocean, that it must be due south, and we should therefore be heading for the western edge of Australia. Any fool could tell which was west, by the setting sun.

Bert reckoned that if we could get up a bit more speed we would take about twelve days to get to the North West Cape. We were moving very slowly, but although we seemed to weave about rather a lot, I managed to keep my bearings.

When it was almost dark, I pulled the mattress diagonally across the bit of deck but could still not stretch out full length. It was better to sit, leaning against the wooden partition of the cabin. A piece of canvas had been lashed roughly across the rails on one side of our 'coop' to screen us from the men on the deck below. It did nothing to protect us from the smoke from the funnel which blew thick, black and oily straight down upon us.

Thus began an evening of pure terror.

As Java slowly faded from sight, the sea very calm, the moon rose uncannily large and bright. I began to look around for things we might throw overboard and cling to if we were hit.

There were neither life-belts nor rafts as far as I could see, only an orange box and some narrow drawers in a fitment in the doll-size cabin.

We continued due south. We were heading for Australia without any doubt, I told myself. Looking back, I remember very clearly that brief period of calm, of looking out to sea and thinking about the ease and luxury of life in Singapore. The lovely clothes, the fun, the servants and the few crazy, idle weekends with Morgan. How carefree, exciting and wonderful it had been – but how artificial. I began remembering much further back, the really happy days when I was a child, picturing the green fields behind our house, the sweet cool rain falling and the horses standing half-sleeping under the trees swishing their tails. I dozed.

TWENTY-FIVE

Waking again, I began watching the gentle rhythmic swell of the sea, feeling the ship beginning to roll, counting the beats of the labouring engines. I spoke to Nana but there was no answer so presumed she was sleeping.

A new sound suddenly came to my ears. The sound of distant aircraft. Somewhere not very far away, the enemy had got wind of activity in the tiny port. They had been waiting until night for a chance to strike.

By now, I was fully awake and so was Nana who called out to me. There were sounds all around us now, men calling orders, scurrying about. The noise of the planes came nearer and nearer. I pulled Nana protesting from her bunk and made her squat with me, heads down on the cabin floor. I talked to her, trying to sound casual, but my voice shook and my breath was restricted. She began to whimper and I felt the horrible fluttering sensation at the base of my spine and began silently to pray.

The aircraft were overhead now. Two of them, dropping things. The unmistakable high-pitched whine of a bomb growing louder and louder, then another. Sickening waves of terror that begin in the stomach and rise through the head then your ears bursting with the explosions. The boat rocked wildly, knocking screaming men off their feet, Nana on top of me, until a great shuddering gripped and shook us as the ship righted itself in the churning waters.

Breathless and helpless, we hung on to each other and waited. We heard stirrings, shouted oaths, hysterical laughter. The bombs had missed us – had fallen in the water. The pilots of these planes were definitely not the Kamikaze 'Divine-Wind' suicide men who had descended with their 'Tora-Tora!' cries to demolish Pearl Harbor. These were from a less skilled squadron. They had missed our pathetic little ship, but they were coming back. We waited, shivering, sick with fright and anticipation of what was to come. We were to be blown out of the sea. We were to be slaughtered – all and every one of us.

The sounds grew nearer and nearer but this time there was only one plane. It dived and roared down on us and I heard the spatter and rattle of machine-gun fire assaulting my senses, splintering the very air, and then the screams and cries of men, the thuds of falling bodies and objects. The small ship was swinging violently, too late, to starboard. The sound of the aircraft was diminishing and after a few seconds it faded completely.

I crept out and looked down. As the ship swayed I could see where the lines of tracer bullets had lacerated the already crimson shadows. In the cruel moonlight, clear as day now, I saw a soldier sitting, his legs stretched out. Bullets had ripped across his lower abdomen. Blood spurted in great jets from beneath his clutching hands but he was still alive. I could see his mouth moving.

That distant sound began again. I held Nana tightly, trying to cover her belly. If only the tiny unborn baby could be spared. She understood and whispered her thanks to me. We were as close as two human beings could ever be. I began breathing more freely for the sounds were growing fainter. The pilot of the enemy aircraft had changed his mind – or perhaps he had run out of bombs.

Behind us a series of resounding explosions caused the vessel to shudder and lurch wildly once more. I lay down doubled up, grinding my teeth, my mind a blank. After what seemed like hours, Bert came with something tepid in a mug, stroked my head and said. 'It's all over – cheer up. Not likely they'll be bothering us again tonight.'

All told, the incident had lasted less than an hour, but in that time, five men had died. Early the next morning I watched as someone read a piece from a prayer-book and the bodies were thrown overboard. Someone sang 'Land of Hope and Glory'. How I hated that tune. Now for me, and for ever after, it would be associated and intermingled with men's screams. I once read somewhere that Elgar himself didn't much care for the song.

Two of the men killed were plaster cases and already badly wounded, Bert told me. The others were members of the crew, one a young Indian, the only man aboard who knew anything about navigation at sea.

A short while later, Bert came back again with some ship's biscuits, a small slice of corned beef and a jug of strong tea.

He showed me a bucket lavatory further along the deck and brought us another bucket of sea-water to wash in. Good-natured and hearty, he kept up a flirtatious banter with us for the whole of the terrible journey.

Poor Nana couldn't eat anything for she had begun to be very sea-sick. In spite of everything I found myself eating ravenously.

I made her take little sips of tea when it had cooled down, but even that she threw up.

The following morning, a fresh-faced blond young man appeared. He wore Air-Force blue trousers and a dirty white vest. He told us Bert had gone down with a bout of malaria. I asked if he could possibly get some drinking water for Nana, and he said we would all get our daily ration. He returned with about a pint of water and some limes which he said I should give to Nana to suck. Later in the day he brought more biscuits and a small tin of evaporated milk.

For three days Nana couldn't keep anything down at all and whimpered all the time like a child. One night she seemed so feverish and delirious, I thought she was going to die. When I put my hand on her stomach, I could feel the baby kicking and felt such compassion I knew I would do everything in my power to save its life. I spent the whole time looking after her. Cleaning her, mopping up, moistening her cracked lips and all the time talking about the baby – her fine son. It had to be a boy, she had said.

She was soaked through with sweat and yet would start such a bout of shivering that I wondered if she too had malaria. The first time I had to strip her I felt horribly embarrassed. Her outer clothes were always so tarty, I wondered what I might find underneath. Half expecting a rhinestone G-string or phosphorescent tassels on her nipples, I was surprised and touched to find she was wearing quite sensible old-fashioned bra and knickers and a petticoat with broderie anglaise flounces.

The shock of discovering one day that I had lice in my hair was minimal to the horror experienced on finding a different species on the hairy areas of my body. There was no way of fighting this affliction. The small piece of soap wouldn't lather in sea-water, the whole ship was filthy. I gave up begging for the bucket to be refilled.

There were more important things to worry about.

We were taking too long to reach the North-West Cape. Our oil supplies were running low and we had very little food left.

Strangely, on about the eighth day, although very weak and emaciated, Nana began to look a better colour. She got off her bunk and staggered along to the lavatory and then wanted to sit out on deck with me. Her swollen round belly was absurd. We both laughed and patted it, and I congratulated her and made her talk about plans for her son. She ate some biscuit and drank a little of the condensed milk and then she slept for several hours without any sign of the fever.

The hours of boredom were the hardest of all to bear. I asked the captain repeatedly (through Bert or the other man), if I might be allowed to help in any way in any other part of the ship, but the reply was always the same. I never even saw this strange Dutch captain but he must have been a misogynist, for his order 'The women must stay in their quarters' was the only response to my plea.

Daily rations became very small. Half a ship's biscuit, usually soggy around the edges, half a can of evaporated milk and a small cube about one inch square of bully-beef or cheese. The hot sweet tea was replaced by brackish water and once as a special treat we were offered some slithery delicious tinned peaches which Bert had found and hidden specially for us.

Nana needed more water than I as her lips were drier and more swollen. To be thirsty in the tropics is painful. You try to make saliva come into your mouth but there is none. Your tongue begins to stick to the roof of your mouth – the sides of your throat threaten to touch. You are lucky to be distracted by anything to make you forget your thirst, until time for the next small drink.

Monotony is worst of all. The endless square miles of ocean mostly calm now, the dreaded long hours of nothingness. I often thought longingly of the old copy of a *Blackwood's Magazine* I had seen in the deserted consulate. In the tiny cabin Nana found a dog-eared old edition of *The Engineer and Boiler-Makers' Weekly* and this I read many times from cover to cover, inventing word games from it, translating it into French.

One afternoon we heard gun-fire very close. It turned out to be revolver shots. One of the men on deck below had thrown a bottle overboard and they were putting in some target practice. It was good to hear laughter, but someone put a stop to the game.

Bert reappeared from his bout of malaria looking thin and pallid. He told us we should shortly be meeting up with an oil tanker. It would be too bad if we didn't, he added, as we hadn't enough fuel to get us down to Fremantle, the western Australian port. Meanwhile, everyone on board who was strong enough was to be put to work helping to get up some spare barrels of oil from the hold. This was to be done by an old hand-winch which, Bert said, was a devil to operate.

I begged once more to be allowed to help – to take my turn, but Bert, head on one side, with friendly pat and sceptical grin, said 'Over my dead body, love,' and departed.

Next day, as soon as it was light, we all started scanning the horizon for the tanker. All that day we strained our eyes, watching and waiting, but there was nothing except a few sea birds, gulls, I supposed, except for one much bigger bird which might have been an albatross. It followed us and I thought of 'The Ancient Mariner' and wished it would go away.

Soon after the bird did vanish, the ship's engines stopped. We were marooned. Everything was uncannily silent and desolate.

Someone said they could see land and we all looked and there, sure enough, was a blessed pale strip barely visible below the cloud line. I thought land must mean Australia and Australia meant civilisation. It came as a blow to be told that the northern part of that coast was desert.

TWENTY-SIX

Still no tanker, so the mammoth task of bringing up the small reserve of oil from the hold began.

The barrels were hauled up on ropes over pulleys. There were very few men strong enough to do the work. Unknown to us at that time, several others had died and been 'buried' overnight without the prayer-book bit.

I begged Bert when he brought our meagre rations, to ask if I might jump overboard and swim, perhaps manage to scrape off some of the grime.

'Have you taken a look down there, girlie?' he asked. I looked.

The water was thick with something, something fleshy and writhing. Snakes. We were surrounded by dozens and dozens of the intertwined greyish pink serpents, thick as a man's arm and up to about twelve feet in length. They reared their evil heads out of the water in their search for food. The sight was blood-curdling. I did not look again.

Another man died that night and when I thought of his body and the snakes I wanted to die myself, to end the horror. This time we heard the brief ... itterings from the prayer-book and Nana wailed, stuffing her mouth with a painted scarf.

By noon the following day the work on the winch stopped and soon afterwards we heard the old engines starting up. Thick smoke started belching down on us once more and we were moving. The small pieces of biscuit we had now were full of weevils, and the water brown and musty.

For the next few days, I don't remember exactly how many, a sort of comatose resignation overtook me. I had even given up imagining what sort of reception we might get at Fremantle if we ever made the port. We were the very dregs of the refugees and evacuees.

Not for us the benevolent reception committees, the hatted do-gooding matrons who had been so hospitable to our embassy families fleeing in the early days of the trouble. We should have to fend for ourselves.

Nana said she had distant relatives in Perth and that I must go with her to find them. I had no intention of foisting myself on a probably not very well-off family, but appreciated her concern and loyalty. As soon as I was able, I should contact the RAF and everything would be taken care of. There would be definite news of Morgan through the Air Ministry in London.

I tried to picture Morgan's face and failed. This worried me.

When all hope of further survival is gone, a sensation of great peace and weariness overtakes the mind. This was the end. One had reached rock bottom at last. Just to lie all day in deep darkness; never more to be a fugitive to be battered from pillar to post; never any more responsibilities to others or to oneself. Just to lie all day and rest. Rest was enough. All the time I knew it didn't matter – I had escaped from prison, from time and from matter, and was free for ever . . .

The next thing I remember, was rain coming down heavily on my face. Endless rain to be licked and swallowed. Then voices and lights. Voices speaking broad English. Forcing my eyelids apart painfully I saw that we were close up against a stone wall. A quay. We had arrived. In Australia.

In the cabin I could see Nana combing her hair, then hitching up her bra and fastening a broken strap with a safety pin. Men were already disembarking. I judged the time to be late evening. No-one came for us women. We were forgotten.

After about twenty minutes of noise and bustle all around us Bert put his head round the corner and said the captain's orders were that we must wait until someone came to collect us. Bert said he was sorry to leave us but he had to get the badly wounded chaps into hospital. Once he had done this, he might even manage to get back for us himself.

We watched the men on stretchers being carried from the gang-plank onto big Army lorries parked on the dock side; others were climbing into a small bus and then waved as they all drove away.

There were no more sounds from the ship except the occasional creak of old timber.

The only people in sight now were two middle-aged men in bowler hats walking up and down with bundles of papers in their hands as if they were expecting important cargoes. We seemed to be in a backwater and were the only vessel in sight but across an estuary I could see the dim shapes of large ships and cranes.

I heaped all the clothes I could find onto Nana who was shivering pitifully and so weak she could hardly walk.

Still no-one came. After about another hour of this, I decided we should go ashore.

If only Morgan were alive and his ship had somehow come here too and he was waiting for me! I'd be a heroine, I thought sloppily. It hadn't and I was not, I told myself sharply.

It took all the energy I could summon to get Nana and our bags off the ship but I managed it and installed her with our belongings in a little building like a bus shelter and went to get help.

Across the far side of the basin I saw a bus arriving with some dock-workers. I asked one of them how we could get across the ferry and into the town. He listened to my story patiently and, against the advice of all his mates, came back with me to see Nana. She was so much more obviously in need of help than I that he went off to find one of the bowler-hatted men who in turn went into an office and telephoned.

Presently, we were helped into a pilot motor-launch and taken to the main part of the harbour where the gate-keeper found us a taxi.

I thanked the docker profusely and he went away with the man in the motor-launch. I hoped his boss would believe his story as the man had mine.

The taxi-driver wasn't very pleased when I told him I had only Dutch money but after a lot of pleading and arguing, he agreed to drive us into Perth.

I was all for taking Nana directly to a hospital but she became quite hysterical at the suggestion and asked through her sobs that we spend one last night together at a hotel or a boarding-house. She said, after we had both had a good night's sleep in a proper bed, we could decide in the morning what was the best thing to do.

The taxi-man dumped us at a 'Bed and Breakfast' in keeping with our appearances, accepting doubtfully the twenty-guilder note and wishing us luck.

The proprietress, a tall woman in a dressing-gown with a mouth like a gin-trap looked us over, listened without a gleam of interest to our plight, and finally gave us two rooms at the back of the house on the ground floor. She told us there was a transport café down the street where we could get something to eat.

We dumped our luggage, made a show of washing our hands and shuffled off to find the place.

At the sight of the big grubby but comprehensive menu, we both cheered up and grinned. Nana started to giggle and couldn't stop until the food came. Nana wanted fish and chips and I settled for bacon and eggs and a big pot of tea. In spite of her fragile condition she got on better than I. The sight of so much food cut my appetite dead. I found I could only manage the yolk of one of the eggs and some bread, but drank several cups of the strong hot tea.

Came the inevitable moment of reckoning. Confronted with the bill I seemed to draw strength from the food I had just eaten and felt I was damned if I was going to do any more grovelling.

I told Nana very firmly to stay put and wait. I was going out to change some money and would be back.

Out in the street I belched loudly, and made for the first big posh hotel in sight. It was called The Esplanade, so we were still near the wretched sea, I supposed. I turned my head away from the coast line towards the bright lights.

TWENTY-SEVEN

I stood on the pavement shivering and peering through the impressive glass-fronted entrance to the hotel. At the far end of the foyer three men were sitting on stools at a bar. Two of them were in uniform.

Being nudged forward by someone – who was quite sure they wanted to go inside – made things easier for me. I found myself revolving in the frightening door, and propelled onto a sickeningly lush carpet on the other side.

The three men hadn't moved. The one on the right could have been English – fair-haired, in tweed jacket with leather patches and grey flannels – the others were in uniform. On the left, naval, with modest amount of gold braid, the middle one in Aussie Air-Force blue. He had an enormously broad back and sticking-out ears.

For no logical reason I remembered my mother saying, 'Never trust a man with flat ears'. It was a good enough lead. The big man would be the one.

In the moment of hesitation, I caught sight of myself in the mirror behind the bottles and flinched. Worse – far worse than I had thought. A skinny girl in faded navy sweater with huge dark-rimmed eyes in a sallow face, dirty sun-bleached hair looped away from hollow cheeks in untidy bunches.

It was now or never. The barman was eyeing me suspiciously. I touched the hefty man's shoulder and stepped back.

He turned and looked at me, his expression a mixture of surprise and defence.

'I can't explain now, but will you please lend me five pounds and not ask any questions? I'll pay you back tomorrow,' I said, speaking the words slowly, urgently and exactly as I had so carefully planned.

The man continued to stare in silence. I could feel the sweat breaking out on my forehead and my legs beginning to tremble.

He could see for himself that I was filthy, undernourished and overwrought. What he couldn't see was that I had seven hundred Dutch guilders in a pocket in my knickers, lice in my hair and was very near to breaking point.

I prayed that he would somehow sense that I had chosen him and be pleased – that I was genuine and very desperately in need of help.

Still he didn't say anything, but the raking arrogant glance softened, the eyes flickered and a wide rubbery grin made the face nicely clownish.

'You're English, aren't you?' he said. I nodded.

Reaching into a back pocket he handed me a folded note.

'Is there an RAF unit in the town or near Perth? I'll meet you there – '

'There is no British unit, only RAAF. It's slap in the middle of High Street – anyone will tell you,' he said.

'See you there then, this time tomorrow, all right?'

'No. Not there, here. Until tomorrow then.'

'Right, tomorrow. Thank you,' I said and fled back through the revolving doors.

It wasn't the first time I had accosted a man and asked for help, but I had never been in Australia before.

TWENTY-EIGHT

When we got back to the boarding-house, I had a scalding hot bath and scrubbed off some of my filth. Nana didn't bother. She was very wise. It was very difficult to clean the rings of grime off the bath-tub afterwards, and I really didn't look much cleaner.

The next morning, I took Nana to a maternity hospital and from there I was sent on to a clinic where I was given a thorough medical check-up, and the first steps were taken to de-louse me. My hair was cut to within an inch of the scalp and my head dipped into something which smelled of creosote, then they shaved my body and painted me with a blue-staining paste. Being declared a leper would have carried more dignity.

I was very, very thin and bony. I felt like a bicycle. My breasts maddeningly and unaccountably alone had retained their fullness. It was obscene. With arms and legs just skin and bone and hip joints jutting, I looked like a swollen matchstick. The nurses congratulated me good-naturedly on my measurements and I laughed with them but was furious when they allowed some of the young interns to come and look at the extraordinary mammal.

A sister loaned me a hospital night-shirt, some dreadnought bloomers and a raincoat, all of which I had to sign for. She directed me to a bank and a good department store, gave me some hair-wash, a tin of vitamin pills and told me to report back in three days for a further check.

Changing the guilders was no trouble at all, but once in a rather smart store I didn't know how to start my shopping. It was quite cold outside. I seemed to hear my mother saying 'A good cloth coat – that's what you need.' Dragging my eyes reluctantly from pastel suits and trendy slack-suits I made for the coat department.

I settled for a sensible classic redingote of dark blue gabardine with real bone buttons and a tartan lining. I have it still.

The rest was easy. I bought everything I needed in the girls' department as I was, it seemed, a standard Australian twelve year old.

Telephoning the maternity hospital, I was told that Nana was to be kept there for about a week and that the almoner was to make contact with her relatives. I sent Nana my love and a bunch of carnations and only then realised how much I missed her.

For the rest of that day, I strode about the town looking for High Street. If Nana had been with me I certainly wouldn't have wasted so much time. She would have asked the first man she saw, but I felt a new and alarming lack of confidence in myself. Any fool ought to be able to find the High Street of any town I kept telling myself. Eventually, I found it was spelled *Hay*.

The RAAF people were charming, friendly and full of concern for my well-being. The only thing they could do for me however was to try to get me onto a boat for Melbourne where I would be able to contact the RAF. This was what they had been doing for all the RAF personnel who had been coming through.

They had no news whatsoever about ships going north from Java. I might be lucky enough to get fixed up with a ship for Melbourne in about five days time, they told me. I was a 'placky girl', they said. I asked about a room in an hotel. I would like to stay at The Esplanade, I told them.

A short telephone conversation and it was done. Someone came in from an ante-room and asked if I had any objection to talking to the press. Not particularly, I answered, but that the girl I had come over with was a far more colourful and interesting character. There was to be a baby too, I added. Nana would enjoy this, I knew. I gave the name of the hospital.

All I craved was anonymity and news of Morgan.

On my way to the hotel, I bought some make-up and made an appointment with a hairdresser. After I had collected my bag I moved into the hotel with all my parcels and then rushed back to the hair salon.

To my intense surprise, my shorn hair had begun to curl around the ears and after the hairdresser (who was called Albert, pronounced Albaire, and came from Houndsditch) had done his best with it, I looked like Shirley Temple Eton-cropped. My plain good-looking clothes did something to counteract the ingénue effect, I told myself, as I got ready to go down to the bar to meet the man who had lent me money twenty-four hours ago.

Just as I had thought, the big Australian did not at first recognise me. When I introduced myself, he did nothing to disguise his surprise and pleasure at my appearance. I handed over his five pounds and let him buy me a drink. His name was Mike and he was in Transport Command.

I was beginning to enjoy myself.

'I hope you haven't eaten yet. Will you have dinner with me?' were almost his first words. It wasn't till then I realised I still hadn't eaten and was starting to feel light-headed.

'Thank you,' I said and we both laughed, each at our private thoughts.

So, we had dinner that evening and the next and the next, and he told me that he too had to go to Melbourne and had arranged to go on the same boat with me.

It was great, being taken care of. I lapped up all the gloss, the pampering, the compliments, the warmth of a man's affection. Besides, I told myself, his presence protected me from all the other predatory males – and there were plenty of them. A lot of the Army had returned from North Africa. Perth at that time was no place for a girl on her own. The streets were full of wandering drunks. Soldiers trying to adjust to the crazy Australian drinking hours.

Sometimes, early in the evening, going out to eat or to a cinema, we would see men lying in rows like fallen nine-pins or propped up outside drinking places (I never saw anything remotely resembling a pub) or they came swaying and lunging at you two or three abreast round corners.

It was a frightening experience.

Just as I had accepted my old Groupie's protection in Bandoeng, I grew accustomed to Mike being around.

I suspected he was married and I knew that I had to watch my step. I certainly didn't want to start an affair with a married man. I was not such a fool as not to know what that might involve. High flirtation and brooding guilt was not for me.

One evening, over the table, apropos of nothing at all, I asked, 'How is your daughter?'

I caught him right off guard and he said too quickly, 'Which one?' and then slowly reddened and guffawed self-consciously.

'You crafty little so-and-so. You're asking me if I'm married, aren't you?' he said.

'I know you are.'

'Too right I am, and three kiddiwinks. How did you guess?'

'You look married,' I said gently.

'Fat and tethered, you mean?'

'No, not at all. Just much too nice to have got away,' I said.

'Do you still want me to come on that boat to Melbourne with you? I could always fly,' he asked me.

'That's for you to decide,' I said.

There was a terrible din around us. The hotel was exceptionally full and noisy. He suggested we should order coffee upstairs in my room.

After ringing for the coffee to be sent up, I went into the bathroom and put on some more 'eau de toilette' and immediately regretted it. He would think it was meant to lead him on. I did it in fact because I was always conscious of the strong smell of the blue ointment I was still having to use on my body. It would be just too bad if I really wanted to start a passionate love affair, I thought, as I sipped my coffee and imagined his horror were he to see the ugly stains on my underwear. I began to giggle.

He edged nearer and reached out for me. I pulled my dress down over my knees and shrivelled away from him.

'I'm not going to rape you,' he said, his voice full of concern, 'I only want to make love to you.'

'I'm sorry,' I said.

'Is it because of your husband?'

'The way I feel right now, I couldn't sleep with anyone,' I said. (Oh Morgan! May heaven forgive me for this, because only with you could I forget the blue blotches and the shame.)

Mike picked up my hand and squeezed it, then we just sat there quietly holding hands like an old married couple at the pictures.

Holding hands can be very reassuring.

The next morning he sent me some flowers, freesias I think they were, and a sweet note saying he had been called to Sydney on an emergency. If I happened to get there myself I was to be sure to ring the number below. It ended – 'There's only one of you. Take care, Love Mike.'

I tore up the bit of pasteboard and put the flowers back into their cellophane sheath to take to Nana at the hospital.

Had I heard her on the radio, she wanted to know as soon as I opened the door of the ward.

She had been interviewed by a gorgeous young reporter and had sung a song over the air and it was all fixed up for her to stay with her relatives who owned a thriving butcher's shop until it was time to come back into hospital for her baby's birth, she told me without pausing for breath. Jack, her husband, was alive and a prisoner in one of the better camps, she added as an afterthought. After the baby was weaned, she had plans for opening up in cabaret.

She had already put on pounds in weight and looked as plump and ripe as a peach. Her room was full of flowers and there were piles of pink, blue and yellow baby woollies, little boots and absurd tiny jackets from well-wishers. To use her own words and later the title of a well-known song, 'Everything was coming up rosy.'

We kissed goodbye, both shedding a few tears and promising to keep in touch.

Two days later, I embarked on a ship for Melbourne.

It was very rough going across the Great Australian Bight. A lot of people were sick and much as I longed to go up on deck I found I was too light and weak to risk being blown overboard so had to stay below in the stuffy atmosphere.

Some of the crew were most attentive and kind to me, but for the most part I kept myself very much to myself, reading anything I could lay hands on. I read Morgan's letters over and over. Some of them I knew by heart.

'I made a bad landing this morning. Not terribly bad or spectacular or even worthy of comment, but still a bad landing. I made up my mind to tell you about it to prove that in spite of what you might think, I am only human even if I am pretty infallible.'

'I love you deeply and intensely. When I am with you there's never enough time to thaw and let my mind talk to you in untrammelled fashion. I'm always so afraid I might lose you. Every time I come to you I fall in love with you all over again, only more and more irrevocably. I'm so excited about this thing. It goes on getting better and better.'

'Sometimes, I know you are afraid of me. Don't be. It's only because I am arrogant and because sometimes I get a little drunk. Please stand in front of your mirror without your clothes on, for me. God, how stupid this war is.'

'You must believe that our life together will be impervious to circumstance and to other individuals. I've waited for such a long time for you to rise out of your slough of office routine petty domesticities – to take you through the Elysian fields of life as someone I defer to and never despise.'

I wasn't at all sure where the Elysian fields were and had my doubts about recognising or appreciating them were I led there, but I laughed lovingly every time at every one of his service jokes.

'German pilot on being shot down by a member of an auxiliary squadron and asked if he was hurt when being hauled out of the sea: "Physically no – morally yes! To be shot down by a bloody barrister flying a bloody bi-plane, is more than I can bloody well bear!"'

I had copied out carefully some nonsense verses – 'Singapore Soliloquies', he called them, written by a friend of his in the squadron –

Gin-soaked
Sin cloaked
Sun-drowned
Hell bound
Singapore.

Pay day
Far away
Knees brown
Head down
Can't think
Have a drink
Damn hot.

No pubs
Only clubs
Tiger beer
Very queer
No dames
No fun and games.

Mess pot
VD
ROTB
Bloody bore
Singapore.

etc.

TWENTY-NINE

We arrived in Melbourne in the middle of an air-raid practice. We were given tin hats and shown straight down into an air-raid shelter. It went on for two hours and I got very cross and belligerent.

When at last I was driven to an hotel, I found it was miles away from the RAF Unit and full of drunken American Army officers. Because they had so much more money than anybody else, they were drunk on the hard stuff.

When one of them tried to climb into a taxi with me the next morning, I took off a high-heeled shoe and struck him with it. He was a pale flabby young man. The two-tone chocolate shaded uniform he wore did nothing for him. I felt sure that the wound I had inflicted was the only one he was likely to get during that war. He would probably get a Purple Heart for it.

At the RAF Unit, a beery-faced sergeant showed me into an inner office. The officer who received me was solicitous, ordering tea for me and himself, fetching a more comfortable chair from another room. After I had sat down there was a pause and then he said he had some information for me. He was very sorry about what he had to tell me. I had to prepare myself to be very brave, he said.

He consulted a file, stood up very straight and enunciating carefully, told me that Acting Wing-Commander R. J. Morgan was posted as missing, believed killed.

He was holding out the sheet of paper for me to see, but everything blurred and I closed my eyes. I heard the well-meaning voice droning on. Would I like to apply for a passage back to the UK or would I agree to remain in Australia for the duration?

He waited for me to speak but I couldn't find the right words. Someone brought a cup of tea and asked if I would like to see the Padré. Were they offering him as a substitute or a consolation, I thought profanely.

'No, thank you,' I said. 'You are very kind. I'll be all right. Can I think about the other thing for a bit?'

'Of course. Try to let us know soon,' the young officer said.

Someone found me a taxi to take me back to the hotel but I told the driver to stop when we came to a park at the top of a hill and I paid him off and went and sat on a bench to think things out.

It was a rather ill-tended, bare, scruffy little park but I had it to myself.

Sitting there, watching some pigeons pecking at the gravel, I thought, so this is it. I am a widow. The widow Morgan. I said it out loud in his sing-song voice.

I wondered if there had been snakes in the sea where his body had gone in.

That he had died bravely, I knew. I prayed that he had died quickly.

Whatever I did from now on I would try to live by his standards. I would not lower my sights or settle for second-best. This might be easier to do in England. I didn't like Australia. Everybody was so crass, so physical and without real humour. The women were pretentious, the men too matey by far. The women all wore hats and gloves to go shopping in the town. The waitresses and shop assistants resented an English accent, were offensive.

I blew my nose, put on some lipstick and went back down the hill to tell them I wanted to go back to England as soon as possible. The officer I had to see had gone out and I was asked to wait a few minutes.

There was a piece of paper on his desk which said:

To all Branches of the RAF, RAAF and WAAF.

Schedule of Clothing. Additional issue.
Knickers (winter)   1/10d
    ,,   (summer)   1/7d
Towels, Sanitary   Free.

I wondered what the beery-faced sergeant thought of all this, and what a pity Morgan had missed it.

The young officer came back, glanced at the notice, then at me and blushed. I told him I had made up my mind that I wanted to go back. He said he would do his very best for me and would be in touch.

I went back to the hotel and wrote to Morgan's mother and to my parents.

For ten days more I had to fill in time, waiting until a passage on a ship to New Zealand became available. I spent a part of each day in a Turkish bath. I still felt dirty although the RAF doctor assured me that there was no further cause for concern. He told me to take things easy and eat plenty of the right nourishing foods. I felt well enough physically, but my appetite was very small.

After about a week of Turkish baths I became even thinner and was so feeble I couldn't stand up without holding on to something.

I avoided people. They seemed to irritate or bore me. I preferred to be alone. One rather shy but erudite middle-aged officer at the Unit tried to get me a membership of a literary club in the town centre, but the public library was really all I needed and I begged him not to bother. He offered to take me to a concert but I couldn't animate myself enough to express my appreciation throughout a whole evening and feigned a headache.

A few days later I was sent to Sydney where I stayed in a sleasy commercial hotel run by an unpleasant character who was anti-Maori. On various occasions I heard him dismissing Maori soldiers from the bar. I liked the look of these brown-skinned men, for the most part quiet and unassuming, and it distressed me a lot to see them treated in this way.

Before joining my ship I bought a few more clothes and had my hair re-shaped. It had grown astonishingly fast, almost back to its normal bobbed length. Slowly, I began to put on a little weight. My cheeks filled out so that I looked less noticeably a refugee.

One day, in a shoe shop, I came across a couple I had known slightly in Singapore. They told me how they too had made a solemn pact to meet somehow eventually in Ceylon but had each been sent unknown to the other, to Australia. They had only met up by sheer chance in the same queue waiting for passages to Colombo, outside a shipping office. They had the good sense not to say anything when I told them about Morgan, just looked at the ground and assured me I was doing the right thing in going back to the UK.

When I finally went aboard the liner (a brand new ship salvaged by the Dutch from Sourabaya just before the port fell to the Japanese), I found various Air Force people I had seen around in Singapore or Kuala Lumpur. I still found it difficult to communicate and stayed most of the time in my cabin. When I felt an unbearable claustrophobia I used to go up on deck and find myself an out of the way corner. I used to sit for hours gazing across the bleak sea trying to imagine life in England without Morgan.

Already I dreaded the inevitable reunions with my family and his, the pity, the commiserations. I knew too that I would avoid any place we had ever been together in.

Sometimes, I prayed we would be attacked and sunk. I wanted to die as Morgan had died, yet strangely, when I felt scared below decks, I took care to memorise the life-boat drill and knew I would fight for survival.

I had a beautifully fitted cabin with its own bathroom and was looked after by a Javanese steward who reminded me very much of Rafi at Buitenzorg.

We put in at Christchurch in the Southern Island of New Zealand and stayed a few days while the ship was loaded with a cargo of mutton and tallow for the States.

The New Zealanders were much easier to get on with than the Australians. One dear old lady came to the ship to invite some of us to go and have a meal at her home. She wanted to give me a fur coat, to keep me warm crossing the Atlantic, she said. It was made from dyed black rabbit skins. Genuine lapin, she called it. I didn't accept it, largely because my mother would never believe that it had been given to me by a dear old lady, but partly because I have never cared for wearing animal skins.

After leaving New Zealand we went straight across the Pacific heading for Cape Horn, but soon we had to keep changing course presumably to baffle the submarines. As we neared Tiera del Fuego, we turned right round. Someone explained that we had been warned not to attempt the east coast of South America but to follow the west instead.

We stopped for one night in Colon, went through the Panama Canal and up to New Orleans. There, we were stuck for more than a month. Many times we attempted to leave the mouth of the Mississippi, but each time had to give up and return to the dock.

It was the beginning of the most successful period of the war for the German U-boats. The numbers of sinkings were horrifying. One night I saw five oil-tankers burning, out at sea. We learned later that from three of these, there had not been a single survivor. I also heard that on one of our attempts to get away, we had a torpedo right across our bows.

I only thought about this seriously, much later on. At the time, all it meant was a return to a fabulous hotel – the Monteleone – in a marvellously colourful town of jazz, bars, night-clubs and some strange and amusing Americans. It also meant a putting-off of the homecoming I was dreading more and more. Quite apart from this, I had come out of my shell and was beginning to enjoy myself.

I used to sleep all afternoon and go out after dark with various people from the ship, exploring restaurants where you could find the finest French cooking, the boîtes of Canal Street where you could hear the best dance bands in the world. They stayed open all night, as long as there was someone to drink their drinks and listen to their music.

In one of these night-spots I met 'Red'. He was one of a couple of American Navy officers, kicking their heels waiting for their ship. He was tall, gauche, shy, came from Boston and was called Dave Magruder. The nick-name 'Red' was because of the colour of his hair. He had unusually pale skin and lively dark eyes.

One evening we were all talking about the Americans coming into the war. I began to listen intently to what 'Red' had to say. He was enormously pro-British and he was making sense, but that wasn't the reason I was drawn to him. It's funny, the things a man says that are truly like him. The moment, in the middle of an ordinary conversation when you suddenly hear the real man talking.

Red and I began to be friends. There followed a succession of crazy, hilarious days and nights such as I had never dreamed could be.

THIRTY

There was an indefinable something about Red that reminded me of Morgan, and this revitalised me.

He made me talk about Morgan and I found I was able to. He listened gravely and didn't say anything. Gradually I began to relax and feel more sure of myself.

We danced and danced, and sometimes for whole evenings just sat silent, listening to the marvellous trumpet-playing.

He took good care of me and when he thought I should go back to my hotel, always insisted on buying me coffee and a fried-egg sandwich at a coffee stall on the way, before seeing me safely back to the door of my room.

This routine went on for several nights. Occasionally he would ring me and come and collect me in the morning and take me to a snobby country club of which all serving officers were honorary members, for a game of badminton or just a walk in the park.

Sometimes he called me 'Mouse-face'. At first I was puzzled, resentful, but soon it became my favourite endearment.

He told me something about himself. He was only a reserve sailor but had seen some action in the Philippines and had been wounded in the left arm which was partially paralysed as a result. His ship was having an overhaul somewhere along the river basin, and he was on indefinite leave pending recall.

In real life he was a schoolteacher. He had a very learned, absentminded father, and a temperamental, rich, bossy mother. His parents were separated, not divorced.

Red was not sure what he wanted to do with his life after he left the Navy, but thought he might go on teaching for a while and finish the book he was writing about rock-climbing which was the only thing he cared passionately about.

I believe there is a threshold of love. I have a low threshold. If I am drawn to a man, I am almost always a bit in love with him by the time I have agreed that it's a fine night for a walk because if I wasn't, I shouldn't be doing so.

In my bed at night, I used to wonder often if Morgan would have liked Red, and I felt sure that he would.

One night or rather very early one morning after a night round the town, Red took me back to my hotel and at the door of my room, drew me close, bent and kissed me.

It was nothing – just a light pressure of the lips.

'Goodnight, little one,' he said and walked away.

When I woke the next morning, the first thing I remembered was the kiss. It probably meant nothing to him, but I had needed it so much.

Later, I felt ashamed of myself and reproached myself for being so easily distracted into being disloyal to Morgan.

The next day, I was aloof and cold. Red looked hurt and puzzled. Each time he came anywhere near me, I felt myself freeze, even the skin of my face stiffened. The right cheek nearest to him grew taut with exposure to his presence.

The poise of his head, the heavy shoulders and especially the eyebrows, the tangle of curly hair reminded me more and more of Morgan. It was an explosive situation.

In one of the night-clubs that night, Red played the piano. He played beautifully with a small group and clowned along with the clarinet player who was improvising. It was great and the crowd went mad and wouldn't let him stop. I had no idea he was so talented, could be so funny, and felt very proud.

After he came back to the table, we danced to a slow blues number. His arms were right around me and now all the fight, all the rejection and conflict were destroyed.

There was no need to speak. He buried his lips against my hair and as we moved to the beat, I felt him trembling.

Don't say anything, I thought. Don't speak. But he did. With his mouth against my cheek, he said, 'It's like nothing that ever happened to me before. I want you so – '

I was scared but yet felt very near to something, some elusive lovely happiness.

We went on with a party of people to other boîtes and it was dawn before he took me back to the Monteleone.

When he tried to kiss me, I drew away and he didn't persist.

'I want to marry you,' he said. 'I think we are right for each other.'

'Don't rush me, I'm pretty mixed-up. I think I love you too – but I have to have time to think.'

He looked into my eyes and smiled his slow-burn smile.

'I want to try to explain – ' I began.

'I shall stop you,' he said.

'How?'

'Like this,' he said and put his mouth against mine for a very long time.

Wrenching myself away was an agony, but I did, and went into my room quickly, shutting the door behind me.

Inside my room I sat down and spoke sharply to myself. I looked in the mirror and reminded myself that I was basically a sensible girl – neither frigid nor wanton, with a good control of my emotions. I must be tranquil for a while, do nothing irrevocable.

I didn't see him the next day. He had left a note at the desk saying he was in agony waiting for my answer, that he had been sent off on a course to a place he was not able to name. I was to be sure to contact him at the Boston address he had given me, if we left for New York.

I missed him terribly and then as soon as I heard we were due to sail, not so much, in the excitement of going back on board and sailing out into the Caribbean.

New York was a disappointment. The other passengers and I stayed in a cheap hotel full of shady business men transacting shady business. I was running short of money and felt like one of the Bisto kids pressing my nose against the windows of Saks and Tiffanys. I missed Red more in that big alien city and was overjoyed when I wired him and got a reply within hours. He could get leave, he said, and would be with me within twenty-four hours.

He arrived the following evening. He could stay only eight hours, but in one week's time was due for fourteen days' leave. He looked so scrubbed, clean and wholesome, and in his haste had cut himself shaving. I felt very close to him and made him let me bathe the gash and put antiseptic lotion on it. We made love.

It was as if life had come back at last to my limbs and as we loved and struggled and panted, I knew that I needed it as much as he did. After a long time I slept, a deeper, different sort of sleep from the sleep of the past months. When I woke, he had gone but there was a huge bunch of tea-roses on the bedside table and a note with three words and his name.

By this time, I had made up my mind. I would marry him.

'You must meet my folks,' he had said earlier. 'I know you'll like the old man – if my ma takes a liking to you, we'll be rich – if she doesn't, we'll be poor – '

We would be poor without much doubt, I thought, but I wouldn't care. I could get a job. After the war Red could go back to teaching.

I would never walk through Morgan's Elysian fields now. I would be pushing a pram in Little Rock or somewhere in the Middle West. Red had said he wanted lots of babies.

Maybe with Morgan I had set my sights too high. I was a very ordinary person. I would have ended up disappointing him. Only one thing was I certain of, at that time. I was unbearably lonely. I could not continue alone. I could not face all my relatives alone.

Would what I was about to do, have called forth Morgan's scorn and derision? Or would he have understood? Was I in fact taking the easy way out, settling for second-best?

In the shabby hotel lobby I asked for a piece of writing paper to draft a note to the adjutant who looked after the Air Force passengers. I had to tell him that I was leaving the ship and staying in America.

Instead of a sheet of paper, the porter handed me a cable just arrived. It was from England, and signed 'Father'. It said:

MORGAN FOUND ALIVE AND KICKING IN HOSPITAL
NEAR BOMBAY GOD BLESS YOU BOTH SAFE RETURN
LOVE.

I slumped down on some steps, closed my eyes, opened them and read the thing again. It said exactly the same.

I felt numb inside but knew that I had to jerk myself into action. I asked the quizzical porter for a telegram form and very slowly and painstakingly wrote a message to Red, telling him not to come back, but to wait for my letter.

I didn't see him again.

Before sailing from New York, I wrote and told him what had happened and he replied at once, addressing the letter to me on the ship. It was a wonderful, sad and funny letter. Among other things he said that wherever I went, I must know that all his love and blessings would go with me and would I please, when I felt able, write to him. He would, he said, like to hear the end of the story. I never did of course, for, as long as one lives, nothing is ever over.

On the ship the purser brought me a letter from my father. In it he told me what he had heard from the Air Ministry about Morgan.

The hospital ship had been torpedoed somewhere off the coast of Sumatra. After being in the water several hours, the survivors had been picked up by a tanker which had taken them to Goa, where Morgan had been unconscious, unidentified for a considerable period of time. Later, he had been transferred to another better equipped hospital near Bombay, was operated on many times by an exceptionally clever Jewish surgeon, recovered his memory, and made known his position to the authorities. He was now on his way home in convoy. My father had once managed to speak to him on the telephone at the last hospital. The line had been very bad and all my father had been able to make out was that Morgan 'had had a terrible trip – very wet – rained all the way.'

I cabled my father the approximate date of my arrival in the UK, but was not allowed to mention the port.

The luxurious innards of the ship had been ripped out and was now full of invasion barges for the landings in Europe.

In the Atlantic we were all wakened at dawn and made to put on life-jackets and go on deck. Those dawn experiences, expecting to be torpedoed at any moment, were hair-raising. I tried to concentrate on my feelings for Morgan. I had been deeply attracted to Red, but knew in my heart of hearts that I would have been settling for second-best. Morgan was my man.

Another less serious, aspect of the long, frightening journey was that I developed quite a taste for Navy rum – much stronger and with quite a different taste from shop-bought!

In a copy of the *New York Times*, several days old, I noticed one morning a bit about the capture by the Japanese of Rangoon and how they planned to build a rail-road to link Thailand with Burma. For this, they would use prisoners from the camps in Malaya and the Dutch East Indies as labourers, it said.

I thought about Rob and hoped that he had died fighting rather than suffer the horrible degradations of a white coolie.

We landed at Gourock one foggy evening in June. I telephoned home from a hotel in Glasgow. My father, his voice vibrant with pent-up emotion, told me Morgan had already arrived and was in London. They were expecting him to ring later that evening to see if there was any news of me. I gave my father the hotel number and waited.

There was a train which would get me to London by morning but I still hadn't got all my luggage off the ship. Unfortunately, when Morgan's call did come through very late, I was at the docks claiming the missing pieces. The message he had left said simply 'The Antelope, Sloane Square, one o'clock.'

I managed to get all my stuff together and catch the train. It was crowded, dirty and arrived in London the next morning very late. I took an uncomfortable bath in the station hotel and changed into the least crushed of my summer dresses. After parking my mountain of luggage in the cloakroom, I found a taxi to take me to our rendezvous. The driver was new to the job and didn't know the way to Sloane Square any better than I. It was almost half-past by the time we turned off Eaton Square.

THIRTY-ONE

As soon as I pushed open the door of the mahogany brown bar, I saw him at the far end. In his so familiar slightly faded blue uniform, a massive line of ribbons on the left breast under the brevet, he looked magnificent. He looked older, battered, but the dog-honest eyes were laughing in a face like an old passport photo I had once seen of his father. There were two knobbly sticks leaning against the bar. Morgan didn't move from his bar stool as I went towards him.

Putting my bag and gloves on the smooth wood, I eased myself up onto the seat beside him. He made no move to kiss me. I didn't know what to do. My face felt stiff and burning, but in the mirror I looked ghastly white, moved beyond my normal blushing.

A fat black cat appeared from nowhere and sat near and started to wash its face. I am incurably superstitious, I knew that meant everything was going to be all right. Morgan as always exuded calmness and vitality.

I felt Morgan's hand go over mine, possessing, imprisoning it. His hand was brown and hard and unchanged, freckled, with the tiny tufts of hair which I loved so much, below each knuckle. I felt tears pricking the backs of my eyelids.

'You're late!' he said, and grinned. 'My widely travelled Chuffie! What would you like to drink?'

Seeing a piece of lemon in his glass I gathered he was drinking gin and tonic, so I said, 'The same as you, please.'

'Large or small gin, sir?' the barman asked.

Morgan and I replied simultaneously. I said 'Large', he said 'Small'. The barman looked back at me and nodded.

'So, it's like that, is it?' Morgan said.

'Yes,' I said defiantly, 'it's like that.'

We laughed together then. His top lip was harder, thinner than it used to be.

I looked down at the sticks and surreptitiously at the thigh a few inches from my free hand. I wanted to touch his leg, to feel for myself, to find out if there was tin or flesh under the barathea.

Morgan was watching me, reading my thoughts, his eyes going over my face as if it had been a page in a book.

I wasn't going to ask any questions yet. His answers were bound to be facetious, either about his wounds or his medals. I tried to make out the bits of ribbon for myself and failed. 'Spam' and 'fruit salad', he would probably say.

Sipping my drink slowly, I began to breathe more freely and relax. Nothing material mattered now. We had all the time in the world to work things out. We could start living – taking up where we had left off. I had made it. I was in the only place in the world I wanted to be, with the only man I really cared about in the whole world.

I had come a long way mentally as well as geographically. We had both come a long way – by very different routes.

He reassured me very simply and gently that he still had both his legs but warned me that he walked with a very bad limp which would go in time.

He changed the subject abruptly. He had heard at the Air Ministry that Rob had died in Changi prison camp. He added that this had strengthened his own resolve to be put back on operational flying in Europe as soon as possible. I winced at this. The war here was at its height. For us, the testing time had really only just begun, but I was ready now. I loved this man with all my heart and I was no longer afraid of him. We had both changed. Only I knew which of us was the stronger character.

Morgan had arranged for us to stay that night at a small hotel in Ebury Street. We seemed to drink an awful lot that first evening, at least Morgan did. He went on ordering wine at dinner and I tried to stop him. I didn't want him to wake after our first night together with a hangover, but the wine certainly helped break down our constraint.

Alone at last in our room, quite suddenly the months of separation and frustration slid away and we were back – looking at the stars.

It was wonderful to enjoy a man so much and to know that he belonged to me.

Waking the next morning, he turned to me, his eyes shining, 'It's crazy – all that hooch and yet I feel like a lion – great – high as a kite – '

'It's called *love*,' I said, burying my face in his shoulder, 'and it's non-alcoholic.'

THIRTY-TWO

I knew that I had to tell Morgan about Red, but I had to wait a while, pick the right time. Whenever I thought about Red I felt a kink in the chest. I had to have the courage to speak out and face Morgan's reaction soon.

After we had spent a short time with our families, Morgan hired an old car and we went to stay on a remote farm on the Welsh border in Shropshire.

Apart from Morgan, the only things I remember about the place are the sun and light and the gentle warmth, the calves, goslings and the rich red earth, the trees shining in their lush summer green.

There was a pony called Rosie which Morgan made me ride round the paddock. I wasn't very good and took a good old toss. He fussed over me, picking me up, and despite his bad leg, carrying me up the stairs to our rooms.

He sat me down on the edge of the bed and smoothed back my hair. 'Now, tell me,' he began, 'tell me about all the men you slept with while you thought you were a widow. Mardi Gras in New Orleans! Wow!'

So, this was it. At once, 'There was someone,' I almost shouted, 'an American – I thought I loved him . . .'

'Oh no!' he cried out, his face drawn with pain. He hit me without warning then, not across the face but on the shoulder like someone trying to knock open a door.

'There is no point in lying to you – I would have told you sometime . . .'

He hit me four or five times more – but not so hard. I doubled over, shielding my head, whimpering a little and ventured to look up at him. The skin of his cheeks looked angry, mottled, the lower lip and eyelids quivering, and I saw tears brimming in the steel-blue eyes. 'Hell!' he said softly, then dropping to his knees tried to cradle me in his arms, to lift me.

'What about you in all those months?' I asked, my mouth against his chest.

'One of the nurses at the last hospital,' he said, 'just once – '

'Was she better than me? Was she pretty – did you love her?'

I listened to my own voice sounding waspish, brittle.

'It wasn't like that. She was old, middle-aged, fat. I started by being grateful – she taught me to walk again, like a kid. She was wonderful – then when I knew she wanted me to make love to her – it seemed right. I doubt if I'd recognise her again now if I saw her on the street – '

'She must have loved you,' I said, and imagined the big plain woman caring for Morgan, putting up with his insolence, his demands and felt a sort of compassion for her.

We both sat up and looked at each other levelly, silently, then he got up and swept me into his arms and threw me across the bed.

It was as if the war, the journeys and the separation had never happened, just that we were older, more knowledgeable. We made love with a rage, then more sweetly and finally gently, almost spiritually, before lying satiated and tranquil in each other's arms.

Perhaps we are all too ready to read history in a complacent book instead of living it. Living history is bound to be full of pain and bitterness. But so, I was soon to find, is the process of birth.